FORM BREAKERS
FOR THE FLAT

FORM BREAKERS FOR THE FLAT

Andrew Mount

Peter Stavers

Published in 2003 by Raceform Ltd
Compton, Newbury, Berkshire RG20 6NL
Raceform is a member of Trinity-Mirror plc

A catalogue record for this book is available from the British Library.

ISBN 1-904317-13-8

Designed by Sam Pentin
Printed by Bookcraft Ltd, Midsomer Norton, Bath

CONTENTS

About The Authors

Andrew Mount

Andrew is a freelance sports journalist and odds compiler. He also works on-course for a major Tatts layer (Martyn of Leicester). He wrote the best selling *Trend Horses: Form-breakers for the Jumps and All-Weather Flat* with Peter Stavers and co-wrote *SprintLine 2002* with Graham Wheldon and Dave Renham. His weekly Trend Horses column can be found on the gg.com website, he has a monthly column published by *In The Know* magazine and previews racing and other sporting events for William Hill's weekly newsletter.

He regularly publishes his findings on Internet forums, including www.finalfurlongracing.co.uk and www.trftalk.com; he has also contributed to *Raceform Update* and *Racing & Football Outlook*. He can be contacted by email at andy.mount@ntlworld.com

Peter Stavers

Peter publishes his analysis and systems on Internet forums, such as www.finalfurlongracing.co.uk and www.directracing.com, and has contributed articles to *In The Know* magazine. A large part of his time is devoted to compiling speed ratings that he uses in conjunction with his form-breaking methods.

INTRODUCTION

Andrew Mount

This book contains the detailed career analysis of over 150 racehorses for the forthcoming Flat season (including all runs up to the end of February 2003). By breaking down their past form and identifying what I consider to be their ideal requirements, I hope to unearth a number of profitable bets.

Distance and going are obvious starting points when studying form; Tara's Emperor, for example, has won three times from three starts at five furlongs on heavy ground. However, the ideal requirements of most horses tend to be rather more complicated than this.

Noticeable preferences may include one or more of the following: the need for a small or large field, for a very recent outing or a long absence between races, for a certain class of race, for a flat or undulating course, for only a short trip to the racecourse, for a right-handed or left-handed track or for a draw near to a running-rail.

As with my last book, *Trend Horses*, I have tried to avoid the obvious selections, and instead have included many lesser lights. You are far more likely to find the winner of a Leicester seller within these pages than this year's Derby winner.

Dandy Regent is a good example. A nine-year-old who hasn't scored outside of selling or claiming company for five years is not the most obvious inclusion for a horses-to-follow book. However, he has an excellent record under very specific conditions. When given a distance of seven furlongs or further, on good or softer ground, when running fresh (after a break of five weeks or longer) in selling or claiming company his record becomes: 113211 (4-6).

I'm expecting that a profit will be made from backing the featured horses under their ideal conditions this season but if forced to choose just ten to follow I would select these:

BARALINKA (IRE)
BE MY TINKER
DUBAIAN GIFT
FOLLOW FLANDERS
GOLDEVA
MADAM MAXI
MATERIAL WITNESS (IRE)
MINDEROO
NORTHSIDE LODGE (IRE)
SIR DESMOND

CHAPTER I
Form-breakers (A-K)

Andrew Mount

A ONE (IRE)
Distance: 5f-6f: 632457045 (0-9); 7f: 50010710 (2-8); 8f: 28 (0-2).
Going: G-F or faster: 3247007 (0-7); Good: 552 (0-3); G-S: 65401 (1-5); Soft / Heavy: 01 (1-2); Fibresand: 0 (0-1); Polytrack: 8 (0-1).
Track: Straight: 32455415021 (2-11); Turning: 60700780 (0-8).
Class: D+: 250700 (0-6); E: 6345 (0-4); F: 172 (1-3); G: 450810 (1-6).
Combine a distance of 7f-8f, on good or softer ground, on a straight track and his record becomes: 51021 (2-5). In class F or lower his figures improve to: 1021 (2-4). From left to right: 1st, 10th – poorly drawn in stall 1 and raced down the stands' side at Leicester (the first three finishers were drawn in stalls 10,19 and 11 of 19, and all raced on the better ground up the centre of the track).

ABBAJABBA
Distance: 5f: 6047822 (0-7); 6f: 250066631131045293001000083020 (4-30); 7f: 69 (0-2).
Going: G-F or faster: 600663000080 (0-12); Good: 27631193003 (2-11); G-S: 5408612 (1-7); Soft: 0522 (0-4); Heavy: 1240 (1-4); AWT: 9 (0-1).
Combine 6f, on good or softer going and his record becomes: 25066311104529 3100320 (4-21).
He failed to score last season but raced on unsuitably fast ground or was poorly drawn on several occasions.

ALLINJIM (IRE)
Distance: 5f-9f: 984273 (0-6); 10f-11f: no runs; 12f+: 141612 (3-6).
Going: G-F or faster: 84162 (1-5); Good: 71 (1-2); G-S: 931 (1-3); Soft / Heavy: 24 (0-2).
Field Size: 10 or more runners: 9827146 (1-7); 9 runners or fewer: 43112 (2-5).
Combine a distance of 12f or further, in a small field and his record becomes: 112 (2-3). His big field win came in a low-grade handicap at Beverley where he was favoured by a high draw (the first three finishers were drawn in stalls 12,10 and 11 of

15). Given his front-running style and propensity to hang to the left in his races he'll be best suited by small fields on left-handed tracks.

ALMAYDAN

Distance: 7f-10f: 43 (0-2); 12f: 23 (0-2); 14f: 11 (2-2); 16f+: 67 (0-2).

Going: G-F or faster: 3167 (1-4); Good: 2 (0-1); G-S: 1 (1-1); Soft: 4 (0-1); Fibresand: 3 (0-1).

Fresh *(after a break of five weeks+):* 432117 (2-6).

Combine a distance of 12f or further, when fresh and his record becomes: 2117 (2-4). From left to right; 2nd by a neck, 1st , 1st and 7th – unable to dominate and absence since this run suggests that he picked up an injury during the race.

ALPEN WOLF (IRE)

Distance: 5f: 56573948170 (1-11); 6f: 877843511101327105320100606528027314441248845200 (8-48); 7f: 10361380088679226 (2-17).

Going: Firm: 1100 (2-4); G-F: 55737448111332753172113860528812484 20 (7-37); Good: 8735900610608685 0 (1-17); G-S: 00 (0-2); Soft / Heavy: 6800 (0-4); AWT: 679273221444 | (1-12).

Field Size: 15 or more runners: 8784940070080006050880671484520 0 (1-32); 14 or fewer runners: 56537735811111363215317211306289273221444268 (10-44).

Headgear: Visor: 370 (0-3); Blinkers: 8 (0-1).

Fresh *(seasonal debut):* 5803 (0-4).

Combine a field size of 14 runners or fewer, G-F or faster ground, no headgear, at any distance, on his second run of the season or later and his record becomes: 58111113 3251721 1328228 (8-22). He has placed first, second or third in 16 of his last 20 starts under these conditions..

Both his seven-furlong wins came on turning tracks (Epsom and Warwick) in slowly run races, he is far better suited by six furlongs.

AMERICAN COUSIN

Distance: 5f: 0025000024214090787511954961581900000090771010136000 (7-52); 6f: 3338001520991842000 94 (2-21); 7f: 0 (0-1).

Time of Year: January to May: 0009054849000090 (0-16); June: 0080217096125974 (2-16); July: 33325421587819710 13 (4-19); August: 000245910060 (1-12); September: 1190000 (2-7); October to December: 00 (0-2).

Fresh *(absence since last race):* 11 days or more: 0300825000022090708595449890000997600 (0-37); 6-10 days: 330425471118611000000130 (6-24); 1-5 days: 01199254710 (3-11).

Combine a recent run (ten days or fewer since his latest start) when racing in the months of June to September and his record becomes: 1421549711196125100047 10130 (9-27). At five furlongs only his record improves slightly to: 4214711961510 0710130 (7-20).

ASHLEIGH BAKER (IRE)

Distance: 7f-9f: 7567903007 (0-10); 10f: 1869457602200086704 (1-19); 11f-12f: 364311243048800 (2-15); 13f+: 79456680 (0-8).

Going: G-F or faster: 73631680030 (1-11); Good: 664037724400087 (0-15); G-S: 589791648648 (1-12); Soft: 190546 (1-6); Heavy: 5022 (0-4); Fibresand: 7000 (0-4).

Combine a distance of 10f, on soft or heavy ground and his record becomes: 1522 (1-4). From left to right: 1st, 5th – poorly drawn at Nottingham and did second best of those drawn in double figures (the first five finishers were drawn in stalls 8,6,14,4 and 13 of 17), 2nd – beaten by a neck and 2nd – beaten by a neck. He goes particularly well at Ayr and ran well there on all three visits last season despite encountering the wrong going: 6th (of 18) on good to soft ground, 7th (of 16) on good ground and 4th (of 20) on good to soft ground.

ASHLEIGH BAKER

ATAVUS

Distance: 6f: 30 (0-2); 7f: 5121110310581857 (6-16); 1m: 1358077014470 (2-13); 1m1f+: 480 (0-3).

Going: Good or faster: 314183580024114137010581857 (7-27); G-S or softer: 5770100 (1-7).

Fresh (seasonal debuts): 5403 (0-4).

Field Size: 9 or more runners: 5311835007701241140070058857 (5-28); 8 or fewer runners: 481311 (3-6).

Combine 7f runs, on good or faster ground, excluding seasonal debuts and his record becomes: 1211110581857 (6-13). In fields of 8 or fewer runners his figures improve to: 111 (3-3).

ATAVUS (right)

ATLANTIC ACE

Distance: 5f: 7 (0-1); 7f: 11103 (3-5); 8f: 180330028 (1-9); 9f: 810 (1-3).

Going: G-F or faster: 71310280 (2-8); Good: 31 (1-2); G-S: 00 (0-2); Soft / Heavy: 1801 (2-4); AWT: 38 (0-2).

Fresh *(after a break of six weeks+):* 7131102 (3-7).

Course: Goodwood: 1321 (2-4).

Combine a distance of 7f or further, on turf, when fresh and his record becomes: 11102 (3-5). The "duck-egg" was excusable as he was badly drawn in stall 18 in the Lincoln Handicap at Doncaster last season. The second-placed effort was a narrow defeat (by a head) in the 21-runner William Hill Mile at Goodwood, a track where he has yet to run a bad race from four outings.

ATLANTIC ACE

AUTUMNAL (IRE)

Distance: 5f: 3112604425035 (2-13); 6f: 234471 (1-6); 7f+: 8896 (0-4).

Going: Good or faster: 12396716442503 (2-14); G-S: 3148825 (1-7); Soft / Heavy: 40 (0-2).

Class: A: 2348896726044503 (0-16); B or lower: 3114125 (3-7).

Combine 6f or shorter, G-S or faster ground, class B or lower company and her record becomes: 311125 (3-6).

BABY BARRY

Distance: 5f: 02236233133000 (1-14); 6f: 40203430307131781480528014540 (4-28); 7f: 7580938 (0-7).

Going: Firm: 33380545 (0-8); G-F: 43358132814 (2-11); Good: 201033017148005 (3-15); G-S: 64270 (0-5); Soft / Heavy: 02807090 (0-8); AWT: 23 (0-2).

Track: Flat: 2324012034308938878005280 0 (1-26); Undulating: 02633703350701311 401454 (4-23).

Headgear: Blinkers: 012 (1-3); Visor: 301317148528540 (3-15); No Headgear: 022362 3470343033580709388000 (0-28).

Combine a 6f trip, good or faster ground, when wearing headgear, excluding flat tracks and his record becomes: 131141454 (4-9). He only once failed to reward each-way support from nine starts under these conditions and that run can be forgiven as he was hampered.

BALI ROYAL

Distance: 5f: 2824212113121652031177 0337 (7-26); 6f: 8704130 (1-7).

Going: Firm: 122 (1-3); G-F: 7813031700337 (2-13); Good: 821173 (2-6); G-S: 04161 (2-5); Soft: 222 (0-3); Heavy: 5 (0-1); AWT: 41 (1-2).

Time of Year: March: 4 (0-1); April: 2112 (2-4); May: 21031 (2-5); June: 281177 (2-6); July: 731230 (1-6); August: 8103 (1-4); September: 0237 (0-4); October: 465 (0-3).

Combine a 5f trip on good to soft or faster ground and her record becomes: 81211312162031177 0337 (7-21). Her record improves further when limiting these runs to those within six weeks of her previous start: 12113121031177 0337 (7-18). She seems best in the early part of the season and if we limit her five-furlong fast ground runs to those in the months of March to June her record improves to: 12112031177 (5-11). The "duck-egg" can be forgiven as she was poorly drawn in stall 14 at Chester (the first three finishers were berthed in stalls 3,1 and 5 of 16).

Her six-furlong win came in a poor race on Southwell's All-Weather surface in which she managed to get an easy lead and was never headed.

BANDANNA

Distance: 5f-5f16 1y: 26513566275474441 19118049 (5-24); 6f: 14357064525002830069 (1-20); 7f: 0 (0-1).

Field Size: 12 or more runners: 7006346567504 70284430098049 (0-27); 11 or fewer runners: 142355165225111169 (6-18).

Combine a distance of 5f-5f16 1y, in a small field and her record becomes: 25 15251111 (5-10).

BANDANNA

BANDLER CHING (IRE)

Going: G-F or faster: 335213477646151255 (3-18); Good: 250708 (0-6); G-S: 3 (0-1); Soft: 4 (0-1).

Track: Straight: 32 (0-2); Left-handed: 53534644825 (0-11); Right-handed: 3210777601 515 (3-13).

Fresh *(absence since last race):* 42 days or more: 3571 (1-4); 10-41 days: 53340776448 55 (0-13); 9 days or less: 221360125 (2-9).

Combine good or faster ground, a straight or right-handed track, a very recent run (nine days or less since his last start) and his record becomes: 221601 (2-6). From left to right: 2nd – beaten in a photo-finish at Newmarket, 2nd – narrowly beaten at Folkestone, 1st, 6th – no obvious excuse, 10th – poorly drawn over an inadequate trip at Beverley and 1st.

BARALINKA (IRE)

Distance: 5f: 122 (1-3); 6f: 11488108 (3-8); 7f: 4 (0-1).

Going: G-F or faster: 148200 (1-6); Good: 1 (1-1); Soft: 82 (0-2); Polytrack: 1 (1-1); Fibresand: 41 (1-2).

Fresh *(first two runs each season or after a break of five weeks+):* 14111 (4-5).

Combine runs at 5f or 6f ,when fresh and her record becomes: 1111 (4-4).

BATHWICK BRUCE (IRE)

Distance: 7f: 62104781 (2-8); 8f: 91170 (2-5); 10f: 9 (0-1).

Going: G-F or faster: 628 (0-3); Good: 91 (1-2); G-S: 0 (0-1); Soft / Heavy: 147170 (2-6); Polytrack: 19 (1-2).

Fresh (absence since last race): 35 days or longer: 6104119 (3-7); 34 days or less: 2971870 (1-7).

Combine 7f-8f, when rested for five weeks or longer and his record becomes: 610411 (3-6). From left to right: 6th – would have finished closer but for being hampered on racecourse debut when an unconsidered 33-1 shot, 1st – won a Chepstow maiden, 11th – no obvious excuse, 4th – not beaten far under topweight in a Chepstow handicap, 1st and 1st.

BE MY TINKER

The runs discussed below are those for her current trainer, Mark Buckley.

Distance: 5f-5f 110y: 12221125 (3-8); 6f: 0421 (1-4).

Going: G-F or faster: 1221104225 (3-10); Polytrack: 2 (0-1); Fibresand: 1 (1-1).

She has improved beyond all recognition since joining her new stable. Amazingly, her last run before joining Mark Buckley came when unseating her rider in a novices' hurdle, but sprinting has since proved to be her game. Her only poor run at the minimum trip (when fifth at Redcar) can be forgiven as it was her ninth start in a ten-week period and she was probably in need of a break. She returned to the track seven weeks later to record an easy win on the Fibresand at Southwell over six furlongs and looks set for a good season at five to six furlongs.

BEST PORT (IRE)

Distance: 7f-13f: 00800977847743 (0-14); 14f: 6633295316617 (2-13); 16f: 12716123430410 (4-14).

Going: G-F or faster: 8066377213131612343464616 (5-23); Good: 073400 (0-6); G-S: 073400 (0-6); Soft / Heavy: 0794 (0-4); Fibresand: 97857 (0-5).

Class: C: 02430 (0-5); D: 0873 (0-4); E: 34295431316106617 (4-17); For lower: 0069 76783721741 (2-15).

Combine a distance of 14f or further, on good or faster turf, in Class D company or lower and his record becomes: 66321231161346161 (6-17). At 16f or further his record improves to: 12161341 (4-8).

BEYOND THE CLOUDS (IRE)

Distance: 5f: 526141421991134804500054526071818 0 (7-34); 6f: 6730683280 (0-10); 7f+: 7900 (0-4).

Going: G-F or faster: 773652442191385586018 1 (4-22); Good: 811100440 (3-9); G-S: 0453278 (0-7); Soft / Heavy: 606900020 (0-9); AWT: 9 (0-1).

Headgear: Visor: 58026 (0-5).

Fresh (seasonal debut): 7895 (0-4).

Draw *(position from a right-hand running rail):* 9 stalls+: 69730049384500045207800 (0-23); 4-8: 6586114914003861 (4-16); 3-: 722115218 (3-9).

Combine a 5f trip, good or faster ground, excluding seasonal debuts, without headgear, when drawn 8 stalls or fewer from a right-hand rail and his record becomes: 11421911011 (7-11). The "duck-egg" can be excused as his stall opened late at Epsom. When drawn 3 stalls or less from a right-hand rail his figures improve to: 2111 (3-4).

BID FOR FAME (USA)

Going: G-F or faster: 13052327510325241 (4-18); Good: 70603 (0-5); G-S: 538 (0-3); Soft / Heavy: 0 (0-1); AWT: 029 (0-3).

Field Size: 12 or more runners: 500527060093054 (0-15); 11 or fewer runners: 38137 3252132211 (4-15).

Combine good to firm or faster ground or an artificial surface, with a small field (11 or fewer runners) and his record becomes: 133252132211 (4-12).

BID FOR FAME (USA)

BLAKESHALL BOY

Distance: Under 6f: 3413215921813700455090807026 (5-29); 6f: 403308983077008 (0-15).

Going: Good or faster: 1403213539210781370045508007102608 (5-34); G-S or softer: 3408983709 (0-10).

Field Size: 20 or more runners: 089808050980 (0-12); 12-19 runners: 5931717704500 07608 (2-18); 11 or fewer runners: 34140321333312 (3-14).

Fresh *(absence since last race):* 16 days or longer: 3409098300 (0-10); 9-15 days: 13288 230770450987 (1-17); 8 days or fewer: 41533171050102608 (4-17).

Combine a distance below 6f, on good or faster ground, when racing eight days or fewer since his previous run and his record becomes: 15110501 (4-8). In fields of 15 runners or fewer his figures improve to: 15111 (4-5), with the only defeat coming as a result of a poor low draw at Beverley.

BLUE VELVET

Distance: 5f: 442342120961106243000218594137 (5-30); 6f: 72460000157623370640 034550728 (1-29); 7f+: 6 (0-1).

Going: G-F+: 232090005270038408 (0-18); Good: 44267216730009572 (1-17); G-S: 160164645513 (3-12); Soft / Heavy: 430634007 (0-9); Equitrack: 4 (0-1); Fibresand: 121 (2-3).

Fresh *(absence since last race):* 42 days or more: 4662 (0-4); 15-41 days: 242016767604021508 (2-18); 14 days or less: 432109172400015623034300003485954 71237 (4-38).

Combine 5f on good to soft turf or Fibresand and her record becomes: 112421513 (4-9). From left to right: 1st, 1st, 2nd (found only Monkston Point too good in a 16-runner handicap, the winner was also running under ideal conditions), 4th (narrowly beaten in a Listed race), 2nd (beaten by course expert Piccled at Southwell), 1st, 5th (badly hampered at Sandown and was probably an unlucky loser), 1st and 3rd (ran well from out of the handicap proper in a competitive Newmarket handicap).

BLUE VELVET

BLUNDELL LANE (IRE)

Distance: 5f: 046060450 (0-9); 6f:
2571531900000871930070018048731410090289010 (7-43); 7f+: 073590 (0-6).

Going: G-F or faster: 2571900036001060474531400289010 (4-31); Good: 501008190
81 (3-11); G-S: 3 (0-1); Soft / Heavy: 78 (0-2); Fibresand: 34700709 (0-8); Polytrack:
90590 (0-5).

Class: B: 900 (0-3); C: 10000749308080 (1-14); D: 2530086104541 (2-13); E: 7151070
6473092890 (2-17); For lower: 07130905019 (2-11).

He's clearly no world beater but since the start of the 2000 Flat season his six-furlong
record, in class D or lower company, on good or faster turf is a respectable:
104314128901 (4-12).

BOANERGES (IRE)

Distance: 5f: 14003150820011126000 (4-19); 6f: 427160700860000 (1-17); 7f+: 309 (0-3)/

Going: G-F or faster: 1139310508011260000 (5-19); Good: 46008600 (0-8); G-S:
32074020 (0-8); Soft / Heavy: 9700 (0-4).

Time of Year: April: 011 (2-3); May: 97032 (0-5); June: 11105060 (3-8); July: 398200
(0-6); August: 6000 (0-4); September-November: 4324070860000 (0-13).

Combine 5f, on good to firm or faster ground, when racing from April to June (he has
yet to race in March) and his record becomes: 1115011260 (5-10). From left to right:
1st, 1st, 1st, 5th – "won" the race on the unfavoured stands' side at Ripon (first six
finishers drawn in stalls 18,19,13,16,2 and 17 of 19), 14th – poorly drawn in stall 15 on
the stands' side at Newcastle (the first six finishers raced up the far side and were
drawn 5,4,8,3,7 and 5 of 19), 1st, 6th – beaten by under two lengths in a field of 17
runners and 13th – poorly drawn in stall 11 at Newcastle (first four drawn 2,3,7 and 8
of 17).

Given his poor form from July onwards he invariably starts each season well
handicapped; he was rated as high as 89 last June but was back to a mark of 78 for
his final run of the season.

BOANERGES (IRE)

BOLD RAIDER

Distance: 7f: 8974 (0-4); 8f: 1234351201426458263 (3-19); 9f: 2 (0-1); 10f: 21379 (1-5).

Going: G-F or faster: 044639 (0-6); Good: 8941641 (2-7); G-S: 231287 (1-6); Soft / Heavy: 7135252232 (1-10).

Fresh (first two runs each season or after a break of five weeks+): 89124204619 (2-11).

Course: Windsor: 112613 (3-6); Others: 89712343520442645823729 (1-23).

Combine a distance of 8f or further, good or softer ground, when fresh and his record becomes: 124241 (2-6). Both fourth places came in handicaps of 16+ runners so he has yet to finish out of the frame in six starts under these conditions. His only poor run at Windsor, whether fresh or otherwise, came on good to firm ground. He has only scored once from 23 starts elsewhere.

BOLLIN NELLIE

Distance: 7f-9f: 43546 (0-5); 10f: 758202135 (1-9); 11f-12f: 451219160610211835952 (6-21); 13f+: 60 (0-2).

Going: G-F or faster: 43578291066025595 (1-17); Good: 4451606213180 (3-13); G-S: 1 (1-1); Soft / Heavy: 521132 (2-6).

Fresh *(seasonal debut):* 4490 (0-4)

Combine distances of 11f-12f on good or softer ground, excluding her seasonal debuts and her record becomes: 51216111832 (5-11). On officially G-S or softer going only her figures are: 5211132 (3-7). From left to right; 5th – no obvious excuse, 2nd (of 18) – beaten in a photo-finish, 1st, 1st, 1st, 3rd – hampered in valuable Ascot handicap yet beaten by less than three lengths (ridden by unfamiliar jockey) and 2nd – beaten by a head in 23-runner November Handicap at Doncaster.

BOLLIN NELLIE

BOND BOY

Distance: 5f: 25100733611817271 (5-18); 6f: 4364445201201907 (2-16).

Going: G-F: 642721 (1-6); Good: 434514520170090 (2-15); G-S: 76 (0-2); Soft: 0318111 (4-7); Heavy: 2037 (0-4).

Course: Doncaster: 63117 (2-5); Goodwood: 5221 (1-4).

Fresh *(after a break of 6 weeks+):* 4410347 (1-7).

Combine 5f , on soft or heavy ground, excluding runs when fresh and his record becomes: 231811 (3-6). From left to right; 2nd – beaten in a photo-finish, 3rd – did best of those to race on the unfavoured far side at Doncaster (first six home drawn 22,13,1,16, 18 and 21 of 21), 1st, 8th – poorly drawn at Pontefract, 1st and 1st.

Despite possessing a better strike-rate over five furlongs he won the Stewards' Cup over six last season and can always be considered at Goodwood over the longer trip.

BOND BOY

BRAVE BURT (IRE)

Distance: 5f: 113998712000007114 (5-18); 6f: 38000 (0-5).

Going: G-F or faster: 138720 (1-6); Good: 193800010 (2-9); G-S: 104 (1-3); Soft: 071 (1-3); Heavy: 90 (0-2).

Combine a distance of 5f on good or softer ground and his record becomes: 199810000711 (4-13). Not the most spectacular strike-rate but if we concentrate solely on his 5f runs, on good or softer ground, in the month of July, for his current trainer (David Nicholls) his record improves to: 111 (3-3). For the last two summers he has run in the same two handicaps, at Newmarket and Ascot, separated by just a few days. He won the 0-85 Newmarket event on both occasions before going on to finish second in the more valuable Ascot event in 2000 (on unsuitably fast ground) and then winning it last season. This season the two races are on Wednesday 9 July and Saturday 12 July and he should prove profitable to back in both.

BRILLIANT BASIL (USA)

Distance: 5f: 22 (0-2); 6f: 100 (1-3); 7f: 109 (1-3).

Going: Good: 0 (0-1); G-S: 0 (0-1); Polytrack: 0 (0-1); Fibresand (Wolverhampton): 9 (0-1); Fibresand (Southwell): 2211 (2-4).

There's nothing complicated about his ideal requirements, he simply runs his best races on Southwell's Fibresand surface and has won or finished a close second in all four such starts.

BUDELLI (IRE)

Field Size: 16 or more runners: 563102086222210702804 (2-20); 12-15 runners: 324 59502626228515720 (1-20); 11 or fewer runners: 25382111 (3-8).

His small field runs are worthy of closer inspection; 2nd – beaten in a photo-finish, 5th – hampered yet still only beaten by just over one length, 3rd, 8th – unsuited by first-time visor, 2nd – beaten by a neck, 1st, 1st and 1st.

Two of his wins in larger fields came when drawn towards the outside of the pack; stall 14 of 17 at Pontefract and 13 of 15 at Goodwood. It looks as though he needs plenty of room in his races.

BUDELLI (IRE)

BUNDY

Distance: 5f: 630625 (0-6); 6f: 04131873436415117069732755429130410 (7-35); 7f+: 78470033800069 (0-14).

Going: G-F or faster: 313647005106973094 (2-18); Good: 63741711735069 (3-14); G-S: 8344382720210 (1-13); Soft / Heavy: 006540135 (1-9); AWT: 8 (0-1).

Fresh (*seasonal debuts*): 63162 (1-5).

Track: Stiff (e.g. Carlisle, Hamilton, Newcastle and Pontefract): 34137364451170673025 002913024651 (5-31); Easy: 607188347001330869705490 (2-24).

Class: C+: 070 (0-3); D: 486108970046 (1-12); E: 637317834344701136672504091325 90 (4-32); F: 10533521 (2-8).

Combine 6f with a stiff track and his record becomes: 41373645117732529130410 (5-22). In class E or lower company his figures improve to: 1373451732529131 (4-16). Take out the runs on good to firm or faster ground and his strike-rate improves further to: 17252131 (3-8).

CALCUTTA

Field Size: 13 or more runners: 34701206080608042000545000710909 (2-30); 8-12 runners: 3213951455242 (2-13); 7 or fewer runners: 31111415 (5-8).

Race Value (*to winner*): £20,000+: 47020608060800970550007105942 (1-29); £19,999 or less: 33131213421145451121455 (8-22).

Combine a small field (12 or fewer runners), in races worth less than £20,000 to the winner and his record becomes: 213114511455 (6-13). In fields of seven or fewer runners only his figures improve to: 3111115 (5-7).

CALCUTTA

CANTERLOUPE (IRE)

Going: Good or faster: 13600 (1-5); G-S or softer: 1433610 (2-7).

Fresh *(after a break of six weeks+):* 113610 (3-6); Others: 433600 (0-6).

Combine G-S or softer ground, when fresh and his record becomes: 131 (2-3). The sole defeat coming from a poor draw in a hot Class B handicap at Ascot where he did best of those to race on the unfavoured stands' side.

CAPTAIN'S LOG

Race Type: Handicaps: 75162490845248668425145944800098313430 (3-38); Non-handicaps: 6711121731155131 (8-16).

Field Size: 13 or fewer runners: 67175124952481419427431181331134 (9-32); 14 or more runners: 608466842515100095530 (2-22).

Combine runs in non-handicaps, in fields of 13 or fewer runners and his record becomes: 6711127311131 (7-13).

CHAMPION LODGE (IRE)

Distance: 7f: 0 (0-1); 8f: 211908370021 (3-12); 9f: 0013 (1-4); 10f: 7226 (0-4).

Going: G-F or faster: 0806 (0-4); Good: 11900021 (3-8); G-S: 237022 (0-6); Soft / Heavy: 713 (1-3).

Headgear: Visor: 8037002 (0-7); Without: 21179000122613 (4-14).

Combine a distance of 8f or further, on good or softer ground, when not wearing a visor and his record becomes: 2119012213 (4-10).

CHAMPION LODGE (IRE)

CHARMING LOTTE

Distance: 5f: 3280 (0-4); 6f: 0715013035761313636700402426346 7094 (4-35); 7f+: 30050 (0-5).

Going: Good or faster: 38070000363670040203467 0 (0-24); G-S: 251609 (1-6); Soft / Heavy: 3153356131424 (3-13); AWT: 7 (0-1).

Jockey: Kim Tinkler: 0067004024207094 (0-16); Others: 328073150513035761 3136 363460 (4-28).

Combine a distance of 6f, on G-S or softer ground, when ridden by any jockey except Kim Tinkler and her record becomes: 15133561316 (4-11). On heavy ground only this improves to: 1536131 (3-7).

CLARINCH CLAYMORE

Distance: 9f or shorter: 79500341 (1-8); 10f-11f: 04272043123 (1-11); 12f-13f: 0321 1142203507202331 (4-20); 14f+: 8178012 (2-7).

Going: Good or faster: 950003414080023 (1-15); G-S: 21232 (1-5); Soft: 704221311 (3-9); Heavy: 2 (0-1); Fibresand: 7238114127353007 (3-16).

Combine G-S or softer going with a distance of 12f or further and his record becomes: 212213112 (4-9).

He was suited by the step-up to two miles last season, and that trip, on soft or heavy ground, may well prove to be his ideal conditions. He is capable of running well when fresh; finishing first (demoted to second place) on his 2001 turf debut.

COLLEGE MAID (IRE)

Distance: 5f: 74221234362981218950020007015000 3005200 (4-39); 6f: 4805215984 0130323273506868400671364 (3-35); 7f: 0570364 (0-7).

Going: Firm: 4989838 (0-7); G-F: 21398053705786740 (1-17); Good: 211510320500 056 (3-15); G-S: 7223402201233614 (2-16); Soft: 8565400070000236 (0-16); Heavy: 4201030640 (1-10).

Fresh (*absence since last race*): 29 days or more: 7429008 (0-7); 22-28: 230250 (0-6); 15-21: 24528060 (0-8); 9-14: 41380640705303030651 64 (2-22); 6-8: 28298900720 008603 (0-17); 5: 8155003 (1-7); 3-4: 151532153402674 (3-15); 1-2: 101703 (2-6).

Combine good or softer ground with break of five days or fewer since her latest run and her record becomes: 115150132 10402 (5-14).

CONNECT

Distance: 5f: 2136043960194552614575700683312334 (4-34); 6f: 0059071 (1-7); 7f+: 779 (0-3).

Going: Firm: 97 (0-2); G-F: 1043569194556750068331 3 (3-23); Good: 270021072 (1-9); G-S: 360 (0-3); AWT: 7945341 (1-7).

Field Size: 12 or more runners: 36000460799455260457570068 (0-26); 11 or fewer runners: 2173959117331233 41 (5-18).

Combine 5f with a small field (11 or fewer runners) and his record becomes:

21391133123342334 (4-13). On turf only his small-field figures improve to: 21391133123 (4-11). He can be forgiven his only unplaced effort under these conditions because he ran too freely in first-time blinkers. He recorded his first ever six-furlong victory in February 2003 (Polytrack) when favoured by the seven-runner line-up and he may be capable of scoring at the longer trip on turf this season in a similarly small field.

CORRDIOR CREEPER (FR)

First run of the season: 7780 (0-4).

Second run of the season: 2311 (2-4).

Third start or later: 2178638070036095040210 8 (2-23).

He has an excellent record on his second start each term: 2nd (of 21) beaten by half a length (14-1), 3rd (of 30) beaten by half a length (16-1), 1st (of 19) at Ascot (14-1) and 1st (of 21) at Thirsk (12-1). The first three runs were for Peter Harris. He was switched to Milton Bradley last season and it was satisfying to see the pattern continue with a 12-1 victory. He has only scored twice from 27 starts otherwise, the first time when odds-on favourite for a Brighton Maiden when a two-year-old and last season, when the well drawn 3-1 favourite for a small-field Chester handicap.

COTTON HOUSE (IRE)

Fresh (after a break of six weeks+): 117118 (4-6).

Quite simply he's best when fresh and has recorded four wins, at odds of 5-4, 5-1, 7-2 and 14-1, from his six runs after a lay-off. The first defeat was excusable; he was poorly drawn in stall one at Doncaster yet still managed to finish second of the unfavoured far side group (the first seven finishers were drawn in stalls 10,16, 9, 11, 12, 4 and 1 of 15 (one non-runner)). His only other defeat when fresh came in a hot Listed race at Newmarket towards the end of last season. The *Racing Post* described the contest as "a particularly strong race, value for a Group tag rather than its Listed status" and Cotton House, a 25-1 shot, was probably outclassed.

COTTON HOUSE (IRE)

CROESO CROESO

Distance: 5f: 0931913154 (3-10); 5f 161y – 6f: 30001110 (3-8).

Going: Firm: 9301 (1-4); G-F: 0354 (0-4); Good: 319110 (3-6); G-S: 011 (2-3); Soft: 0 (0-1).

Track: Straight: 093390540 (0-9); Turning: 100131111 (6-9).

Fresh (seasonal debut): 090 (0-3).

Combine good to soft or faster ground, on a turning track, excluding seasonal debuts and his record becomes: 111111 (6-6).

CROESO CROESO

CRYSTAL CASTLE (USA)

Distance: 7f or shorter: 21034111 (4-8); 8f or further: 637 (0-3).

Fresh (seasonal debut): 203 (0-3).

Combine runs at 7f or shorter, excluding seasonal debuts and his record becomes: 14111 (4-5). The sole defeat was excusable as he was badly hampered in The Wokingham Handicap at Royal Ascot.

CRYSTAL CASTLE (USA)

CURRENCY

Distance: 5f-5f16ly: 6002 (0-4); 6f: 001111212050376210045370 (6-23); 7f+: 00 (0-2).

Going: Firm: 125 (1-3); G-F: 00111212314 (5-11); Good: 657620370 (0-9); G-S: 08 (0-2); Soft / Heavy: 000 (0-3); AWT: 0 (0-1).

Class: C+: 0560243708 (0-10); D-: 6000001111212037215 (6-19).

Combine 6f, good to firm or faster ground, below class C company and his record becomes: 01111212315 (6-11).

D'ACCORD

Distance: 5f: 443164246303032436 (1-18); 6f: 015350090068225530 (1-18); 7f+: 000 (0-3).

Going: G-F or faster: 35049032 (0-8); Good: 062000003 (0-9); G-S: 22 (0-2); Soft: 4 (0-1); Heavy: 44668 (0-5); Equitrack: 113 (2-3); Fibresand: 53045330 (0-8); Polytrack: 056 (0-3).

Course: Windsor: 00668222 (0-8).

Fresh *(seasonal debut):* 0500 (0-4).

A poor career strike-rate (two wins from 39 starts) and a zero from 28 return on turf hardly make him an obvious inclusion. However, his Windsor record, on G-S or faster ground, excluding seasonal debuts is: 222 (0-3). From left to right; 2nd (of 22) – beaten in a photo-finish when a 25-1 shot, 2nd (of 22) – beaten half-a-length by fellow course expert Sir Desmond and 2nd (of 23) -again, narrowly beaten by Sir Desmond. The two Sir Desmond / D'Accord Computer Straight Forecasts paid £194.35 and £94.15.

DAMALIS (IRE)

Distance: 5f: 32144166314644446108180061039003 (6-32); 6f: 369355030269769263 750 (0-21); 7f+: 7 (0-1).

Going: Firm: 05 (0-2); G-F: 134446410510337070 (3-18); Good: 346188352629260373 (1-18); G-S: 669660 (0-6); Soft: 213140069 (2-9); Heavy: 4 (0-1).

Course: Chester: 1341131320037 (4-13); Others Tracks: 32441663164644946088055 006030676299267350 (2-41).

Combine a distance of 5f, when running at Chester and her record becomes: 14111 300 (4-8). Given a draw in stall 8 or lower her 5f Chester figures improve to: 14111 (4-5).

Despite her two wins on a soft surface she is almost certainly better on faster ground. Her first soft ground win came at Ripon in a weak five-runner two-year-old Conditions Stakes, where she raced on the favoured stands rail from her stall one draw. She was again favoured by the draw for her other soft ground win at Sandown, where she broke well, grabbed the far rail, and made all the running.

The two races described above are also the only ones that she has won at tracks other than Chester, where she is rightly regarded as a course expert. She has now lost her last 32 starts elsewhere, a losing run stretching back to April 1999. Her 9-4 (favourite) starting price at Leicester last September remains one of the great mysteries of the 2002 Flat season. Laying her on the betting exchanges when she raced at tracks other than Chester proved to be a profitable betting strategy last season.

DAMALIS (IRE)

DANCING BAY

Distance: 7f-9f: 571 (1-3); 10f-12f: 1048760 (1-7); 13f+: 1067131 (3-7).

Going: G-F or faster: 507 (0-3); Good: 71063 (1-5); G-S: 41 (1-2); Soft: 180 (1-3); Heavy: 1671 (2-4).

Field Size: 13 or more runners: 10876703 (1-8); 8-12 runners: 571406 (1-6); 7 or fewer runners: 111 (3-3).

Combine a small field (12 or fewer runners), on soft or heavy ground and his record becomes: 1111 (4-4).

His only big-field win came on a straight track and it remains doubtful that he can handle traffic when racing around a turn.

DANCING BAY

DANDY REGENT

Distance: 6f: 075024457085 (0-12); 7f: 9422186000085110949350021 (4-24); 8f: 30456 0004001600 (1-15).

Going: G-F or faster: 975804094905 (0-12); Good: 04213060511000600 (3-17); G-S: 578211 (2-6); Soft / Heavy: 243540 (0-6); AWT: 2405608000 (0-10).

Fresh (after a break of five weeks+): 0922421135008211 (4-16).;

Class: Sellers: 00254017100025 (2-14) Claimers: 464934110 (2-9); Others: 097542213 0860050850940508060 (1-28).

Combine 7f or further, on good or softer ground, when running fresh in selling or claiming company and his record becomes: 113211 (4-6). From left to right: 1st (10-1), 1st (10-1), 3rd (20-1, hampered and poorly drawn, did best of the single figure stalls in a 22-runner Newmarket claimer – nine of the first ten finishers were drawn in double figures), 2nd (40-1), 1st (8-1) and 1st (7-1).

A nine-year-old who hasn't scored outside of selling or claiming company for five years is not the most obvious inclusion for a horses-to-follow book. However, he has a decent record when fresh and should prove profitable to follow on this season's reappearance.

DANEHURST

Distance: 5f: 111901001 (5-9); 6f: 1123011 (4-7).

Going: G-F: 11200 (2-5); Good: 91 (1-2); G-S: 0131 (2-4); Soft: 11 (2-2); Heavy: 01 (1-2); Fibresand 1 (1-1).

Class: Group 1: 02300 (0-5); Group 2: 91 (1-2); Group 3: 111 (3-3); Listed: 0111 (3-4); Others: 11 (2-2).

Headgear: Blinkers: 1011 (3-4).

Combine runs on good to soft or softer turf (or Fibresand), when racing below Group 1 company and her record becomes: 1101111 (6-7). The sole defeat was excusable on account of her difficult stall 16 draw at The Curragh (the first four finishers were drawn in stalls 7, 4, 3 and 5 of 16).

DANEHURST

DANI RIDGE (IRE)

Distance: 5f: 5 (0-1); 6f: 21681 (2-5); 7f: 63800 (0-5).

Going: G-F or faster: 610 (1-3); Good: 3 (0-1); G-S: 216 (1-3); Soft / Heavy: 580 (0-3).

Track: Straight: 2856800 (0-7); Turning: 1631 (2-4).

Fresh *(after a break of six weeks+):* 211 (2-3).

Combine a turning track when running fresh and her record becomes: 11 (2-2). Pay close attention to her runs at Chester this season, a turning track on which her trainer, Eric Alston, has an excellent record.

DAYGLOW DANCER

Going: G-F or faster: 32590962410 (1-11); Good: 24523590 (0-8); G-S: 002 (0-3); Soft / Heavy: 12621660080 (2-11); Fibresand: 1 (1-1).

Fresh *(absence since last race):* 6 weeks +: 13410192 (3-8); Under 6 weeks: 225226263 5956006024190080 (1-26).

Combine a slow surface (good to soft or softer turf or Fibresand), when rested for six weeks or longer and his record becomes: 1112 (3-4). He has won on all three seasonal debuts to date, at odds of 2-1, 9-4 and 16-1.

DAYGLOW DANCER

DEFINING

Distance: 7f-8f: 636 (0-3); 10f: 117 (2-3); 12f: 1111 (4-4).

Going: G-F or faster: 11 (2-2); Good: 61 (1-2); G-S: 671 (1-3); Fibresand: 3 (0-1); Polytrack: 11 (2-2).

At distances of 10f or further, on any ground his record is: 117111 (6-7). On a fast surface only (good or faster turf, or Polytrack) this improves to: 11111 (5-5).

DEFINING

DERWENT (USA)

Distance: 8f: 93 (0-2); 10f: 339117719 (3-9); 12f: 4 (0-1).

Going: Firm: 19 (1-2); G-F: 33141 (2-5); Good: 7 (0-1); G-S: 37 (0-2); Soft: 99 (0-2).

Headgear: Blinkers: 1417719 (3-7); Without: 93339 (0-5).

Combine a distance of 10f, when blinkered, on good to firm or faster ground and his record becomes: 1119 (3-4). The sole defeat is probably excusable for one or more of the following reasons; 1) it came at the end of a long hard season, 2) he was held up too far off the slow early pace and 3) he goes particularly well on local tracks (he is trained in North Yorkshire) but the defeat occurred at Newmarket. His Yorkshire ten-furlong record on good to firm or faster going is: 33111 (3-5), including three from three when blinkered.

DORCHESTER

Field Size: 13 or more runners: 07009050076000750306243270855 (0-28); 12 or fewer runners: 811123438121 (5-12).

Fresh *(after a break of six weeks+):* 840000 (0-6).

Combine a small field (12 or fewer runners), when returning to the track within six weeks of his latest run and his record becomes: 1112338121 (5-10).

DUBAIAN GIFT

Distance: 5f: 1132151 (4-7); 5f 161y-6f: 4868 (0-4).

Quite simply he has yet to run a bad race at the minimum trip: 1132151 (4-7). From left to right: 1st, 1st, 3rd (possibly needed the run after a four-month break), 2nd (stumbled at the start then raced on the slower part of the track), 1st, 5th (narrowly beaten in a blanket finish) and 1st.

DUCK ROW (USA)

Field Size: 12 or more runners: 6735 (0-4); 8-11 runners: 63073345271550282 (1-17); 7 or fewer runners: 1373161222411 (5-13).

Class: Group 1: 6376 (0-4); Group 2: no runs; Group 3: 02252750821 (1-11); Listed: 723345215 (1-9); Others: 1633117413 (4-10).

Combine a small field (seven runners or fewer) below Group company and his record becomes: 13311241 (4-8).

DUCK ROW (USA)

DUMARAN (IRE)

Distance: 6f: 0 (0-1); 7f: 16301 (2-5); 8f: 510020 (1-6); 9f: 1081 (2-4); 10f: 7 (0-1).

Going: G-F or faster: 030 (0-3); Good: 10180 (2-5); G-S: 1600 (1-4); Soft / Heavy: 57121 (2-5).

Track: Straight: 0150 (1-4); Turning: 1076311002601 (4-13).

Combine distances from 7f to 9f, on good or softer ground, on a turning track and his record becomes: 1061102801 (4-10). On good to soft or softer going his record improves to: 161021 (3-6). From left to right: 1st, 6th – poorly drawn at York, 1st, 10th – given a poor ride by Frankie Dettori at Sandown (usually sits in just behind the leaders but Dettori sent him off in front), 2nd – beaten by a short head at Ascot and 1st.

E MINOR (IRE)
Distance: 6f-8f: 0750 (0-4); 11f-12f: 12309 (1-5); 13f-14f: 62 (0-2); 15f+: 231 (1-3).
Going: Good or faster: 026 (0-3); G-S: 510 (1-3); Soft / Heavy: 702 (0-3); Polytrack: 33129 (1-5).
Fresh *(after a break of six weeks+):* 011 (2-3).
Combine a distance of 11f or further, when fresh and his record becomes: 11 (2-2).

EASTERN MAGENTA (IRE)
Distance: 5f: 43 (0-2); 6f: 13614 (2-5); 7f: 823 (0-3).
Going: G-F or faster: 48 (0-2); Good: 6 (0-1); G-S: 1142 (2-4); Soft / Heavy: 333 (0-3).
Track: Flat: 1361423 (2-7); Undulations: 438 (0-3).
Combine a flat 6f or 7f, on good to soft or softer going and his record becomes: 131423 (2-6). Both wins came at Ayr where he has a two from three career record (hampered and possibly unlucky in the other).

ERUPT
Course: Musselburgh: 1671 (2-4).
Headgear: Blinkers: 6 (0-1); Visor: 391240050 (1-9).
Combine runs at Musselburgh without headgear and his record becomes: 171 (2-3) – the sole defeat excusable as he was badly hampered.

He had developed into something of a Musselburgh specialist for Mel Brittain before switching stables to Sue Wilton. He failed to score for his new handler and even ran over hurdles. He's now back with Brittain and showed much better form last season, winning a soft ground seller at Ayr on his final start. He will always be of interest in sellers, regardless of the track but would be maximum bet material if lining up in one at Musselburgh.

FANTASY BELIEVER
Distance: 5f: 324221692901000609 (2-18). 6f: 0745142131571004800 (4-19).
Going: G-S or faster: 2269127209431514110004800006 (5-28); Soft / Heavy: 2745 03109 (1-9).
Fresh *(absence since last run):* 15 days or more: 3221907923700048 (1-16); 14 days or fewer: 426245140115110 (5-15).
Fresh (first three runs each season): 234745004 (0-9).
Combine a distance of 6f, when returned to the track 14 days or less since his latest start, on his fourth start onwards and his record becomes: 1411510 (4-7).

He began last season with a handicap rating of 95 but after a winless campaign it had dropped to 82. He takes a few runs to come to hand and, hopefully, he'll be down to a mark in the high seventies by the time of his fourth start this season.

FANTASY BELIEVER

FAR LANE (USA)

Distance: 6f: 7 (0-1); 7f: 1 (1-1); 8f: 2423 (0-4); 9f-10f: 4522 (0-4).
Going: G-F or faster: 2423522 (0-7); Good: 7 (0-1); G-S: 1 (1-1); Soft: 4 (0-1).
Fresh *(after a break of six weeks+):* 7122 (1-4).

He very much caught the eye when first home (second overall) of the unfavoured stands' side (low) in the Cambridgeshire at Newmarket last backend (first eight drawn 26,2,23,33,35,22,34 and 28 of 30 (five non-runners)) and should progress from handicap to Listed or Group company this season.

FAR LANE (USA)

FLAK JACKET

Distance: 5f: 300002130000734I2400800543005 (2-29); 6f: 70117902601102I031166 (7-21); 7f: 0000 (0-4).

Going: G-F: 031021I300224316300 (4-19); Good: 7902001010001465 (3-16); G-S: 760004005 (0-9); Soft: 0007318 (1-7); Heavy: 100 (1-3).

Time of Year: March: 7 (0-1); April 730 (0-3); May: 03700000 (0-8); June: 19003 (1-5); July: 102112412514 (5-12); August: 0213041016 (3-10); September: 600000360 (0-9); October: 000005 (0-6).

Combine 6f or shorter in the months of June to August and his record becomes: 11902211I302412410351 (8-21). At 6f only, during the same period his record improves to: 1190211021031 (6-13). When running within five days of his previous start his figures improve further to: 11121 (4-5). He has won the Stewards' Sprint Stakes at Glorious Goodwood for the last three years and will no doubt be aimed at the race again this season.

FLY MORE

Going: G-F or faster: 5150473881I1006006416009 (5-24); Good: 554052 (0-6); G-S or softer: 40826 (0-5).

Field Size: 14 or more runners: 155004380820600506200 (1-21); 13 or fewer runners: 45578111464169 (4-14).

Fresh (absence since last race): 6 days+: 4551550047380860 600506246009 (1-28); 5 days or fewer: 8111421 (4-7).

Combine his runs in small fields (13 or fewer runners), on G-F or faster ground, after a very recent run (5 days or fewer since his last outing) and his record becomes: 1111 (4-4).

FOLLOW FLANDERS

Distance: 5f: 11546 (2-5); 6f: 05 (0-2); 7f: 0 (0-1).

Going: G-F or faster: 15506 (1-5); Good: 4 (0-1); Heavy: 0 (0-1); Polytrack: 1 (1-1).

Fresh (after a break of six weeks+): 115 (2-3).

Like two of her dam's other offspring, Speed On and Kyllachy (both also trained by Henry Candy), she goes very well when fresh on a fast surface at five furlongs. She's definitely one to support on her seasonal debut.

FOOL ON THE HILL

Distance: 6f-9f: 064285086 (0-9); 10f: 2151165 (3-7); 11f: 2 (0-1); 12f: 23 (0-2).

Going: G-F or faster: 20861653 (1-8); Good: 212 (1-3); G-S: 0452 (0-4); Soft / Heavy: 6851 (1-4).

Fresh (first two runs after a break of eight weeks+ or after a break of four weeks+): 0642850221112 (3-13).

Combine a trip in excess of 9f, when running fresh and his record becomes: 221112 (3-6). He was a 25-1 winner on his reappearance last season and first time out may be the best time to catch him.

FOREVER TIMES

Distance: 5f: 218 (1-3); 6f: 362304071431042224546 (2-21); 7f: 3709121662200084 (2-16).

Going: Firm: 21146 (2-5); G-F: 32892162830224 (1-14); Good: 613674245 (1-9); G-S: 7201400 (1-7); Soft / Heavy: 3040 (0-4).

Field Size: 13 or more runners: 6137040091266207008304245 (2-25); 12 or fewer runners: 322831214122446 (3-15).

Class: B+: 3742704546 (0-10); C: 830926620481042224 (1-18); D: 32200103 (1-8); E-: 6111 (3-4).

Combine any distance, in class C or lower company, on good or faster ground and her record becomes: 36221839121662831042224 (4-23). In small fields (12 or fewer runners) her form figures improve to: 32281122 (2-8). The eighth-placing can be forgiven on account of a difficult draw (stall one over five furlongs at Beverley).

Her only win on ground softer than good came when favourite for an Apprentice Classified Stakes, a race in which she was favoured by the weights and started as the 7-4 favourite. She is better suited by fast ground.

FOREVER TIMES

FOURTH DIMENSION (IRE)

Distance: 8f-12f: 490020 (0-6); 14f: 21115325 (3-8).

Going: Firm: 02115 (2-5); G-F: 92132 (1-5); Good: 45 (0-2); G-S or softer: 00 (0-2).

Course: Yarmouth: 111 (3-3); Others: 49002025325 (0-11).

Combine a distance of 14f (one and three-quarter miles) on good to firm or faster ground and his record becomes: 2111325 (3-7). At Yarmouth only his form figures improve to: 111 (3-3). Although yet to win at any track other than Yarmouth he was only beaten by a short head on firm ground at Redcar last season.

FOURTH DIMENSION (IRE)

FULL SPATE

Distance: 5f: 07 (0-2); 6f: 500360541039404030810037709111550014 (6-36); 7f+: 2345310060903020156050990 (2-25).

Going: G-F or faster: 6009063513440310030201560091150I (6-32); Good: 2310004090085750 (1-16); G-S: 5500 (0-4); Soft / Heavy: 43300991047 (1-11).

Combine 6f and good to firm or faster going and his record becomes: 0651344031003 7911501 (5-20). He ran his best races last season when drawn on or near a favoured running rail.

GENERAL HAWK (IRE)

Distance: 5f: 8 (0-1); 6f: 38058 (0-5); 7f: 012401001 (3-9); 8f: 4041415 (2-7); 9f: 0 (0-1).
Going: Firm: 8045 (0-4); G-F: 051241010101 (5-12); Good: 3084 (0-4); G-S: 8 (0-1); Fibresand: 04 (0-2).
Track: Left-handed: 040111 (3-6); Right-handed: 84001 (1-5); Straight: 388051240405 (1-12).
Class: D: 080244415 (1-9); E: 385001801 (2-9); F: 10410 (2-5).
Fresh (seasonal debut): 300 (0-3).

Combine a distance of 7f-8f, on good to firm or faster ground, excluding seasonal debuts and his record becomes: 12441010115 (5-11). Although not the most consistent of animals his starting prices of 8-1,6-1,10-1,12-1 and 9-2 made up for the occasional poor run.

GOLDEN BRIEF (IRE)

Distance: 6f: 7 (0-1); 7f: 00850841546101018660045416101032 (8-33); 8f: 33005543 (0-8); 9f+: 4 (0-1).

Going: Firm: 010 (1-3); G-F: 436034 (0-6); Good: 08487 (0-5); Soft / Heavy: 00 (0-2); Equitrack: 3 (0-1); Fibresand: 85000 (0-5); Polytrack: 154561015645416101132 (7-21).

Fresh *(absence since last race):* 9 days or longer: 003850844300145601008660004745460032 (2-35); 8 days or less: 51131111 (6-8).

Class: C: 003 (0-3); D: 0035405362 (0-10); E: 50431560118660044541111 (6-22); F: 8840171 (2-7); G: 0 (0-1).

Combine a distance of 7f, when running on Polytrack or fast turf (good to firm or faster) in class E or lower company, when returned to the track 8 days or fewer since his last race and his record becomes: 111111 (6-6).

GOLDEVA

Distance: 5f: 12722 (1-5); 6f: 225193 (1-6); 7f+: 60 (0-2).

Going: G-F or faster: 12609 (1-5); Good: 2222 (0-4); G-S: 57 (0-2); Soft / Heavy: 13 (1-2).

Fresh *(days absence since last run):* 42+: 1213 (2-4); 41-: 222572609 (0-9).

She has yet to finish out of the frame in four starts when rested for six weeks or more and is clearly best when fresh. Six furlongs on a soft surface also suit and she has only faced these conditions twice after a sufficient break. In the first of them she won a valuable (£25k to the winner) handicap at Ascot and in the other, finished third of 19 behind course expert Tom Tun when a 25-1 shot for a Doncaster Listed race on her final start of the season. A return to Doncaster for the Cammidge Trophy on Lincoln Day would be an ideal starting point in what should prove to be a successful campaign.

GOLDEVA (left)

GOODENOUGH MOVER

Distance: 6f: 6106 (1-4); 7f: 71142904302821112 (5-17); 7f 122y+: 609014228000 (1-12).

Going: Good or faster: 66001111429042208002211110 (7-25); G-S or softer: 7904386 (0-7); AWT: 62 (0-2).

Track: Straight: 761111490403082821162 (6-20); Turns: 609024220010 (1-12).

Runs for Previous Trainer *(G F H Charles-Jones):* 676090 (0-6).

Combine good or faster ground, when running on a straight track, since joining his current trainer (J S King) and his record becomes: 11114900822112 (6-14). At 7f his figures improve to: 111149022112 (5-11). The three poorest efforts can all be excused; 4th – involved in prolonged duel for the lead, 9th – poorly drawn (finished second in his group), 11th – went off too fast when ridden by an inexperienced apprentice jockey.

HOLLYBELL

Distance: 5f: 5910821350 (2-10); 5f 161y+: 354130179 (2-9).

Going: Firm: 919 (1-3); G-F: 3101 (2-4); Good: 5307 (0-4); G-S: 50 (0-2); Fibresand: 8 (0-1); Polytrack: 21345 (1-5).

Track: Flat: 58213451017 (3-11); Undulations: 59310309 (1-8).

Combine a 6f trip, on a flat track, on G-F or faster turf and her record becomes: 11 (2-2).

HOLLYBELL

INCLINE (IRE)

Distance: 5f: 0 (0-1); 7f: 3813; (1-4); 8f: 6471 (1-4).

Going: G-F: 478 (0-3); Good: 3 (0-1); G-S: 0 (0-1); Soft / Heavy: 113 (2-3); Fibresand: 6 (0-1).

Combine a distance of 7f or 8f, on G-S or softer ground and his record becomes: 113 (2-3).

With only nine career starts to his name we don't have a great deal to go on but the way he improved when encountering soft ground and a straight track at seven furlongs to a mile suggests that these will be his ideal conditions.

INTERNATIONAL GUEST (IRE)

Distance: 5f: 0 (0-1); 6f: 052 (0-3); 7f: 437 (0-3); 8f: 613301 (2-6); 10f: 1 (1-1).

Going: G-F or faster: 053 (0-3); Good: 423 (0-3); G-S: 0670 (0-4); Soft / Heavy: 3111 (3-4).

Headgear: Blinkers: 54263011 (2-8); Visor: 7133 (1-4); Without: 00 (0-2).

Combine a distance of 8f or further on soft or heavy going and his record becomes: 111 (3-3).

INTRICATE WEB (IRE)

Distance: 6f: 0 (0-1); 7f: 5931606135062121120207105584680 (7-32); 8f: 50373906 026454 (0-14); 9f: 0 (0-1); 10f: 6110 (2-4); 11f+: 7 (0-1).

Fresh *(absence since last race):* 1-20 days: 630113375390620067508260 (2-24); 21 days or more: 595600602111121058460011 7454 (7-29).

Combine a distance of 10f, when returning to the track three weeks or longer since his latest outing and his record becomes: 11 (2-2). Despite his good strike-rate at seven furlongs he is better suited by longer distances nowadays. He may be capable of winning at twelve furlongs this season.

IONIAN SPRING (IRE)

Distance: 7f-8f: 30020 (0-5); 9f-10f: 212044016115396 (4-15); 11f-12f: 2150 (1-4); 13f+: 7 (0-1).

Going: G-F or faster: 2207139 (1-7); Good: 307065 (0-6); G-S: 1 (1-1); Soft / Heavy: 160 (1-3); Fibresand: 120215 (2-6); Polytrack: 44 (0-2).

Fresh *(after a break of 6 weeks+):* 3207200119 (2-10).

Trainer: Lord Huntingdon: 3221 (1-4); Charlie Egerton: 007204421507 (1-12); Clive Cox: 161153960 (3-9).

Since joining his current trainer, Clive Cox, he has proved best when fresh on a soft surface. He did manage to win on officially good to firm ground at Chepstow on his debut for Cox but that came in a weak race where the final time of the race suggested that the ground was softer than the official version. He's definitely one to support on his seasonal debut.

IONIAN SPRING (IRE)

ISLAND LIGHT

Distance: 8f: 721120851 (3-9); 9f: 0 (0-1).

Going: G-F or faster: 7105 (1-4); Good: no runs; G-S: 2281 (1-4); Soft: no runs; Heavy: 10 (1-2).

Fresh *(first two runs each season or after a break of five weeks+):* 721201 (2-6).

Combine a distance of 8f, when running fresh on good to soft or softer ground and his record becomes: 221 (1-3).

ISLAND LIGHT

J M W TURNER

Distance: Distance: 5f: 600725 (0-6); 6f: 531975101100005711 4245 (6-22); 7f: 462240 (0-6).

Going: Turf: 653197451000000072557 (2-21); Polytrack: 612402 (1-6); Fibresand (Southwell): 44 (0-2); Fibresand (Wolverhampton): 1115.

Headgear: Blinkers: 5106214014245 (3-13); Visor: 1100722557 (2-10); No Headgear: 65319746000 (1-11).

Combine 6f, on Wolverhampton's Fibresand surface, when wearing headgear and his record becomes: 1115 (3-4). The sole defeat by fewer than two lengths after meeting trouble in running.

JAMESTOWN

Distance: 5f: 052 (0-3); 6f: 05 (0-2); 7f: 14614421010044647057 (4-20); 8f+: 6084734091070000 (1-16).

Going: G-F or faster: 0050461004 (1-10); Good: 2607075 (0-7); G-S: 1400 (1-4); Soft / Heavy: 14844 (1-5); Fibresand: 5214730496100 (2-13); Polytrack: 07 (0-2).

Fresh (after a break of five weeks+): 0101441470 (3-10).

Headgear: Visor: 6 (0-1).

Combine a distance of 7f, on a slow surface (good to soft or softer turf, or Fibresand), without headgear and his record becomes: 14421014 (3-8). He goes very well when fresh and won his only start under these conditions after a lay-off.

JASMICK (IRE)

Field Size: 12 or more runners: 3340600 (0-7); 8-11 runners: 744725645 (0-9); 7 or fewer runners: 11 (2-2).

She is unbeaten in two small-field starts, both on right-handed tracks. The first when a 6-1 shot at Salisbury (1m4f), the second when 10-1 for a Kempton handicap last season (1m6f). She has run well at York before and it may just be coincidence that both wins came on right-handed courses.

JAWHARI

Distance: 5f: 0100071791521213123 (6-19); 6f: 2400260639351142 (2-16); 7f+: 105000 (1-6).

Going: G-F+: 210520213113 (4-12); Good: 000616091242 (2-12); G-S: 0000 (0-4); Soft: 49 (0-2); Heavy: 0 (0-1); AWT: 7171353215 (3-10).

Fresh (first two runs after a long break (four months or more) or break of 6 weeks+): 2410 00001071132131 1 (7-19).

Combine 5f, good or faster ground or an All-Weather surface, when running fresh and his record becomes: 107112111 (6-9). From left to right: 1st, 0 – poorly drawn in stall 4 at Goodwood (first three drawn 17, 13 and 14 of 17), 7th – All-Weather debut and poorly drawn on the inside at Wolverhampton, 1st, 1st, 2nd -beaten in a photo, 1st, 1st and 1st.

JESSICA'S DREAM (IRE)

Distance: 5f: 1101151733030 (5-13); 6f: 511237 (2-6); 7f: 6 (0-1).
Going: G-F or faster: 561130750 (2-9); Good: 1173330 (2-7); G-S: 2 (0-1); Soft: 1 (1-1); Heavy: 11 (2-2).
Combine a distance of 5f, on soft or heavy ground and her record becomes: 111 (3-3). Although she has won on fast ground and at six furlongs she has not done so since graduating from handicap company.

JEWEL OF INDIA

Distance: 5f-6f: 34 (0-2); 7f: 451 (1-3); 8f: 1157311 (4-7); 9f+: 53 (0-2).
Going: G-F or faster: 347 (0-3); Good: 455 (0-3); G-S: 11 (2-2); Soft: 1 (1-1); Polytrack: 13 (1-2); Fibresand: 513 (1-3).
Headgear: Blinkers: 1153513 (3-7); Without headgear: 3454171 (2-7).
Combine a distance of 7f or 8f, on good to soft or softer going and his record becomes: 111 (3-3).

JOOLS

Distance: 6f: 140188 (2-6); 7f: 410400 (1-6); 8f: 8114506520 (2-10); 9f: 0 (0-1); 10f: 66 (0-2).
Draw (number of stall positions from a favoured rail – 6f runs only): 1-2 stalls: 141 (2-3); 3-6 stalls: no runs; 7 or more stalls: 088 (0-3).
He improved for the drop to six furlongs last season and ran well the three times he was given a draw on or near a favoured rail; winning at Windsor and Newmarket either side of an unlucky run when badly hampered at Windsor.

JUST JAMES

Distance: 6f: 10146 (3-5); 7f: 610 (1-3).
Going: G-F or faster: 1160 (2-4); Good: 0 (0-1); G-S or softer: 614 (1-3).
Field Size: 12 runners or fewer: 66 (0-2); 15 runners or more: 101410 (3-6).
Fresh (seasonal debut): 60 (0-2).
When only considering his runs in big fields, excluding his seasonal debuts his record becomes: 11410 (3-5). The "duck-egg" can be forgiven as he was poorly drawn on the far side (high) in The Tote International Handicap at Ascot (first six finishers drawn 13, 1, 5, 4, 7 and 6 of 28).
Seven furlongs may prove to be his best trip as his six-furlong wins came in low-class races and/or on stiff tracks.

KING'S IRONBRIDGE (IRE)

Distance: 6f: 2 (0-1); 7f: 15186170 (3-8); 8f: 10436 (1-5).

Fresh *(first two runs each season or after a break of five weeks+):* 211810631 (4-9); Other runs: 54760 (0-5).

Class: Group 1: 80 (0-2); Group 2: no runs; Group 3: 116 (2-3); Listed: 54376 (0-5); Others: 2110 (2-4).

Combine a distance of 7f-8f, when running fresh, below Group 1 company and his record becomes: 2111631 (4-7).

KING'S IRONBRIDGE (IRE)

KNOCKEMBACK NELLIE

Distance: 5f: 768900121005097028905310295250060600000 (3-40); 5f110y – 6f: 020 24505750307 (0-14); 7f: 85 (0-2).

Field Size: 13 or more runners: 800459050070007080530520000360600000 (0-35); 9-12 runners: 76825259299007 (0-14); 8 or fewer runners: 2115125 (3-7).

Combine a distance of 5f with a small field (8 or fewer runners) and her record becomes: 11125 (3-5). From left to right; 1st, 1st, 1st, 2nd – by a head and 5th – hampered and eased.

CHAPTER 2
Systems

Peter Stavers

Amateur rider system

The minimum weight carried in races consigned to amateur riders is 10st instead of the usual 7st 10lbs. This is because the average amateur is bigger and heavier than the average pro-jockey. Topweights in amateur rider handicaps often have to carry 12st. Logically, this should count against them but these horses actually perform better than the topweights in normal races, who are allotted no more than 10st.

Amateur rider handicap topweights – 13.25%
Ordinary handicap topweights – 12.64%

Not a huge difference admittedly but enough to show that the extra burden is no hindrance. Backing the two highest weighted horses in amateur rider handicaps, who were carrying more than 11st and who were sent off at odds shorter than 4-1 would have produced pleasing results:

1994-2002
Amateur rider handicaps
SP less than 4-1
Weight carried greater than 11st
Top two in the weights

249 runs
80 wins (32.13%)
+34.09 LSP (Level Stakes Profit)
+13.69 ROI (% Return on Investment)

Penalty carrier system

Horses that win a race and then reappear in a handicap before the official handicapper has time to adjust their handicap rating have to carry a weight penalty. It's understandable that trainers often prefer to run their winners under a penalty as not only are they in peak condition but they also could well face a bigger increase in their rating than the penalty they've incurred.

Good profits can be made by following these penalty carriers under certain conditions – back all penalty carriers that reappear within seven days, that had been off the track no more than 15 days prior to their win last time, and are in the first four of the betting forecast:

1996-2002

Penalty carriers
In the first four of the betting forecast
Last ran less than eight days ago
Absence from the track before their previous run of less than 16 days

416 runs
136 wins (32.69%)
+181.47 LSP
+43.62 ROI

Quick return winners system (non-handicaps)

Non-handicap races are usually won by in-form horses, especially those around the head of the betting. Backing last-time-out winners contesting non-handicap races (sellers excluded), who are returned to the track within seven days, and who are sent off either first or second favourite produces decent profits:

1995-2002

Winner last time out
SP (starting price) favourite or SP second favourite
Last ran less than eight days ago
Non-handicaps (sellers excluded)

697 runs
278 wins (39.89%)

+76.20 LSP
+10.93 ROI

Mick Channon System

Trainer Mick Channon has a cracking record with his runners that were narrowly beaten last time out:

1998-2002

Beaten less than one length last time out.

223 runs
50 wins (22.42%)
+59.52 LSP
+26.69 ROI

His runners in claimers and sellers are well worth following too, especially those that are sent off at odds of less than 10-1.

1998-2002

Claimers and sellers
SP less than 10-1

194 runs
50 wins (25.77%)
+44.38 LSP
+22.88 ROI

A P Jarvis System

Alan Jarvis does far better with his older horses than he does with his younger ones. His runners aged four or older are profitable to follow when dropped in class, especially when towards the front end of the betting market:

1995-2002

Age 4yo or older
SP less than 6-1
Dropped in class since from last start

170 runs
31 wins (18.24%)
+83.00 LSP
+48.82 ROI

His runners aged four or older are even more profitable to follow when racing in class D or lower company if they finished third or worse last time out:

1997-2002
Age 4yo or older
Class D or lower
Finished third or worse last time out
273 runs
41 wins (15.02%)
+136.66 LSP
+50.06 ROI

David Nicholls System

Runners from the stable of Dandy Nicholls must be given plenty of respect when they run on southern tracks. His record with older horses is far better than that of his younger ones, and he clearly specialises in races over shorter distances.

Backing all his runners aged five or older at tracks south of Newmarket, over trips shorter than 1m1f and that are sent off at odds shorter than 8-1, would have produced impressive results over the last few seasons:

1997-2002
Age 5yo or older
Courses south of Newmarket
SP less than 8-1
Distance less than 9f

226 runs
70 wins (30.97%)
+99.44 LSP
+44.00 ROI

W M Brisbourne System

This trainer is a dab hand at getting back-to-back victories out of his horses, especially on turf when their outings are no longer than 15 days apart:

1999-2002
Winner last time out
Last race fewer than 16 days ago
Turf racing only

43 runs
14 wins (32.56%)
+51.00 LSP
+118.60 ROI

J R Fanshawe System

James Fanshawe has an impressive record when he takes just one horse to a meeting, and when they are near the front end of the betting market they are very profitable to follow:

1998-2002
Trainers' sole runner at meeting
SP less than 8-1

404 runs
119 wins (29.46%)
+104.17 LSP
+25.78 ROI

J H M Gosden System

When John Gosden has a runner in a two-year-old maiden that is sent off favourite you should sit up and take notice, the chances are that it will win:

1995-2002
2yo maiden races only
SP favourite

143 runs
73 wins (51.05%)
+32.84 LSP
+22.97 ROI

P W Harris System

Peter Harris has a tremendous record with his runners in all-aged handicaps. Had you backed every single one of his 859 runners blindly in such races over the last five seasons you would have made a profit (3.79 ROI). That's an incredible statistic considering the sheer volume of runners.

However, there is a distinct difference in his record in races for certain age groups. You would have lost 26.21% of your total stake had you backed just those qualifiers aged five and above whereas backing the younger horses would have produced far better results:

1998-2002

All-aged handicaps
3yo and 4yo runners only

663 runs
71 wins (9.34%)
+83.91 LSP
+12.66 ROI

R Hannon System

When Richard Hannon decides to take just one runner to a meeting, and that horse is either a two-year-old or a three-year-old, he usually means business. Backing all of his runners that fall into this category would have produced a profit in five of the last six seasons:

1997-2002

Trainers' sole runner at meeting
2yo and 3yo runners only

330 runs
64 wins (19.39%)
+63.85 LSP
+19.35 ROI

G Kelleway

Gay Kelleway knows how to get a winner on the sand, and you would have made good profits by blindly backing her All-Weather runners in maiden races during the last five years:

1998-2002

All-Weather only
Maiden races

77 runs
16 wins (20.78%)
+105.46 LSP
+136.96 ROI

P J Makin System

This trainer is adept at placing his runners in all-aged handicaps, and often has big priced winners in that sphere. Backing all of his runners in these races, when not raised in class, has proved a profitable tactic over the last few years:

1999-2002

All-aged handicaps
Not up in class from last run

232 runs
31 wins (13.36%)
+129.88 LSP
+55.98 ROI

CHAPTER 3
Form-breakers (L-Z)

Andrew Mount

LADY BEAR (IRE)

Distance: 6f: 63 (0-2); 7f: 34414076 (1-8); 8f: 9211070344134210135 (6-20); 9f: 560 (0-3); 10f+: 400P (0-4).

Going: GF+: 63441900400030 (1-14); Good: 07P611 (2-6); G-S: 2461 (1-4); Soft: 1153 45 (2-6); AWT: 3413472 (1-7).

Combine runs at one mile, on good or softer ground and her record becomes: 2117341115 (5-10). From left to right; 2nd – pulled eight lengths clear of the third-placed horse, 1st, 1st, 7th – unfavourable low draw, 3rd – did best of the low-drawn runners (first four finishers drawn 30,29,11 and 32), 4th – poorly drawn in stall 22 at Doncaster where five of the first seven finishers were drawn in stall 6 or lower, 1st, 1st, 1st and 5th – her first run outside the UK.

LADY BEAR (IRE)

LADY PAHIA (IRE)

Distance: 7f: 40301150061808005 (3-17); 8f: 28630925 (0-8); 10f: 2 (0-1).

Going: G-F or faster: 4311566108080 (3-13); Good: 089 (0-3); G-S: 2003 (0-4); Soft / Heavy: 0 (0-1); Polytrack: 0252 (0-4); Fibresand: 5 (0-1).

Field Size: 13 or more runners: 000806600980052 (0-15); 12 or fewer runners: 43112 531825 (3-11).

Track: Straight: 008800 (0-6); Turning: 43011250663109802552 (3-20).

Fresh (seasonal debut): 406 (0-3).

Combine a small field (12 or fewer runners), a fast surface (good or faster turf, or Polytrack), on a turning track, excluding seasonal debuts and her record becomes: 311512 (3-6). She has won the same Fillies' Handicap, run at Goodwood in June, for the last two seasons and can be backed with confidence if attempting a three-timer this season.

LADY PAHIA

LAW BREAKER (IRE)

Distance: 72221393060402298093805415 (2-26); 6f: 4053033380416119010050010709 (5-27); 7f+: 69172040 (1-8).

Going: G-F or faster: 74380419009038 (1-14); Good: 03042 (0-5); G-S: 90904 (0-5);

Soft / Heavy: 038550 (0-6), Equitrack: 3 (0-1); Polytrack: 69740 (0-5); Fibresand (Southwell): 23216112500 (3-11); Fibresand (Wolverhampton): 53201260101179 (4-14).

Class: C+: 534900504050709 (0-15); D: 703233938060102298095 I I (3-23); E: 03210 0711410380 (4-15); F: 42669142 (1-8).

Combine Fibresand runs below Class C company and his record becomes: 2232160 1216011211 (7-17).

LISIANSKI (IRE)

Distance: 5f: 111835010 (4-9); 6f: 0304 (0-4); 7f+: 000 (0-3).

Going: G-F or faster: 000313450 (1-9); Good: 1101 (3-4); G-S: 080 (0-3).

Headgear: Visor: 3111845010 (4-10); No Headgear: 000003 (0-6).

Fresh *(absence since last race):* 42 days or longer: 035 (0-3); 15-41 days: 0034 (0-4); 14 days or fewer: 011180010 (4-9).

Draw *(position from a favoured rail – sprint runs only):* 3 stalls or fewer: 11 (2-2); 4: 131 (2-3); 5-6: 4 (0-1); 7+: 0380500 (0-7).

Combine visored runs at 5f, when returning to the track within two weeks of his latest start and his record becomes: 111801 (4-6). Throw out the runs when he was not drawn close to a favoured rail and his record improves to: 1111 (4-4).

LOCKSTOCK (IRE)

Distance: 7f: 0012139 (2-7); 8f: 4387133230 (1-10); 9f+: 020 (0-3).

Headgear: Blinkers: 21321390 (2-8); Without: 040038721033 (1-12).

Track: Straight: 381210 (2-6); Turning: 04007210332339 (1-14).

Combine a distance of 7f, when blinkered, on a straight track and his record becomes: 121 (2-3), with the sole defeat by just a short head.

He improved for the fitting of blinkers last season, winning two from two over Chepstow's straight seven-furlong track, one on soft ground and the other on good to firm.

LOOK FIRST (IRE)

Distance: 6f-7f: 231 (1-3); 8f-9f: 261191 (3-6); 10f-12f: 85706227077235795 (0-17); 13f-14f: no runs; 15f+: 214131523147 (4-12).

Track: Left-handed: 23186511706227077279243231457 (4-29); Right-handed: 9351115 (3-7); Straight: 21 (1-2).

Class: C+: 205 (0-3); D: 706777435247 (0-12); E: 8261925113 (3-10); F: 315139211 (4-9); G: 2172 (1-4).

Combine a distance of 15f (one mile and seven furlongs) or further, in class E or lower company and his record becomes: 211131 (4-6). Both defeats were narrow ones, the first by just half-a-length and the second by a head and a neck in a three-way photo-finish. On right-handed tracks his record improves to: 111 (3-3).

LOOK HERE NOW

Distance: 5f: 0 (0-1); 6f: 1500100777718119 (5-16); 7f: 060908627 (0-9).

Going: Good or faster: 1500007708762 (1-13); G-S: 9 (0-1); Soft: 1601 (2-4); Heavy: 07 (0-2); Fibresand (Southwell): 119 (2-3); Fibresand (Wolverhampton): 78 (0-2).

Combine a distance of 6f on good to soft or softer turf (or Southwell's Fibresand track) and his record becomes: 10101119 (5-8). From left to right; 1st, 0 – poorly drawn in stall 16 at Chester, 1st, 0 – poor low draw on last season's reappearance, finished fourth best of the single-figure stalls, 1st, 1st, 1st and 9th – no obvious excuse.

LOOK HERE NOW

LORD PROTECTOR (IRE)

Distance: 6f: 0 (0-1); 7f: 4251300220351 (2-13); 8f: 262479 (0-6).

Going: G-F or faster: 432600 (0-6); Good: 52501 (1-5); G-S: 27023 (0-5); Soft / Heavy: 29 (0-2); Fibresand: 14 (1-2).

Track: Straight: 456207003901 (1-12); Turning: 21324225 (1-8).

Combine a straight 7f on G-S or faster turf and his record becomes: 4500031 (1-7). These figures look average had best but he has often had excuses for the poor runs. From left to right: 4th – not beaten far in a 21-runner Newbury maiden on his race-course debut when an unconsidered 40-1 shot (came out second best of those drawn low), 5th – needed the run to qualify for a handicap mark, 10th – poorly drawn, 10th – poor high drawn in last season's Victoria Cup at Ascot, 10th – poor drawn yet again, this time in the Buckingham Palace Stakes at Royal Ascot, 3rd – hampered and not beaten far in the 17-runner Bunbury Cup at Newmarket and 1st – won a 30-runner Newmarket handicap.

His only win on a turning track came when odds on for a weak Southwell maiden. Granted better luck with the draw he should win one or two decent handicaps this season. He has joined Spanish based trainer Eddie Creighton over the winter but is still expected to race in the UK this season.

LORD PROTECTOR (IRE)

LOUGH BOW (IRE)

Going: G-F or faster: 7070029 (0-7); Good: 70 (0-2); G-S: 11 (2-2); Soft: 72 (0-2).
Headgear: Blinkers: 2291 (1-4); Visor: 14 (1-2); Without: 7077070 (0-7).
Combine good to soft or softer ground when wearing headgear and his record becomes: 121 (2-3).

LUCEFER (IRE)

Distance: 6f: 1 (1-1); 7f: 0292219090720 (1-13); 8f: no runs; 9f+: 09 (0-2).
Going: G-F or faster: 0190 (1-4); Good: 1 (1-1); G-S: 297 (0-3); Soft / Heavy: 22009 (0-5); Polytrack: 20 (0-2); Fibresand: 9 (0-1).
Fresh *(absence since last race):* 42 days or more: 01912 (2-5); 41 days or fewer: 29229 009070 (0-11).
Combine a distance of 6f-7f, when running fresh and his record becomes: 0112 (2-4). From left to right; 12th – saddle slipped, 1st (9-4), 1st (25-1) and 2nd – beaten by a short head (6-1).

LYGETON LAD

Distance: 7f: 090731241 (2-9); 8f: 71110123214 (5-11); 9f: 648 (0-3); 10f: 30132475 (1-8).

Going: G-F or faster: 73131707 (2-8); Good: 014 (1-3); G-S: 0 (0-1); Soft / Heavy: no runs; Polytrack: 231122321514 (4-12); Fibresand: 6491084 (1-7).

Field Size: 16 or more runners: 09311170312 (4-11); 12-15 runners: 1080271232151 (4-13); 11 or fewer runners: 6743444 (0-7).

Combine a fast surface (good or faster turf, or Polytrack) with a big field (12 or more runners) and his record becomes: 3112170731122232151 (7-18). Knock out the runs at distances beyond a mile and his strike-rate improves to: 1170311223211 (6-13). On Lingfield's Polytrack surface only his figures are a very consistent: 311223211 (4-9).

MADAM MAXI

Distance: 7f: 691705 (1-6); 1m: 02105630925602201300 (2-20); 1m1f+: 086 (0-3).

Going: G-F or faster: 602670350 (0-9); Good: 0239516 (1-7); G-S: 910021 (2-6); Soft: 082 (0-3); AWT: 0560 (0-4).

Fresh *(first two runs each season or break of five weeks+):* 692103025221 (2-12); Others: 0085696170060500 (1-17).

Combine runs at 7f-8f, on good or softer ground, when fresh and her record becomes: 921325221 (2-9). For her current trainer only, H.S.Howe, this improves to: 1325221 (2-7). From left to right; 1st, 3rd (beaten in a three-way photo at odds of 33-1), 2nd (by a short head at 50-1), 5th (an outclassed 40-1 shot behind subsequent Group 3 winner Duck Row), 2nd (by a neck), 2nd (by three-quarters of a length) and 1st.

MAGIC FLUTE

Distance: 7f: 75580 (0-5); 8f: P2020634109160090 (2-17); 9f+: 0 (0-1).

Going: G-F or faster: 5P206804006090 (0-14); Good: 7203110 (2-7); G-S: 50 (0-2).

Fresh *(after a break of six weeks+):* 7223091 (1-7).

She has broken blood vessels in the past and usually runs best after a long lay-off. An each-way bet on Magic Flute when running fresh at one-mile would have returned a profit four times out of six: 2nd at 14-1, 2nd at 7-1, 3rd at 25-1 and 1st at 12-1. She has won the same class D handicap, run at Bath in mid-July, for the last two seasons (at odds of 20-1 and 12-1). This year's race takes place on Sunday 13 July and she would be worth betting if attempting the hat-trick, especially if turning out after a lay-off.

MAGIC MISTRESS

Distance: 7f: 515 (1-3); 8f: 954 (0-3).

Going: G-F or faster: 95 (0-2); Good: 1 (1-1); G-S: 5 (0-1); Soft / Heavy: 54 (0-2).

Track: Straight: 95154 (1-5); Turning: 5 (0-1).

She has only six runs to her name but has performed well in the five on straight tracks: 95154 (1-5). From left to right; 9th (of 18) – an unconsidered 50-1 shot for her racecourse debut in a competitive Newmarket Maiden, 5th (of 9) – beaten under two lengths (33-1) despite meeting interference in a Yarmouth Maiden, 1st – won her Maiden at Chepstow where the small field (5 runners) proved ideal, 5th (of 30) – 25-1 for her handicap debut at Newmarket and 4th – did best of those to race away from the favoured far rail in a Doncaster handicap (first four drawn 1,2,7 and 15 of 23).

It's too early to say that she can't win on a turning track but given her knack of meeting trouble in running it would seem that small fields and/or straight tracks are likely to prove ideal.

MAJIK

Distance: 6f: 11441 (3-5); 7f: 006 (0-3); 8f: 00 (0-2).

Going: G-F or faster: 0044 (0-4); Good: 1 (1-1); G-S or softer: 01 (1-2); Fibresand: 1 (1-1); Polytrack: 06 (0-2).

Combine a distance of 6f, on a slow surface (good or softer turf, or Fibresand) and his record becomes: 111 (3-3).

He has performed well in all five starts at six furlongs: 11441 (3-5). From left to right; 1st, 1st, 4th – did best of those to race on the stands' side at Nottingham (the first seven finishers were drawn in stalls 9,4,10,18,11,5 and 6 of 20), 4th – narrowly beaten by three better-drawn rivals at Windsor, and 1st.

MALHUB (USA)

Distance: 5f: 2 (0-1); 6f: 11722 (2-5); 7f: 118 (2-3); 1m: 95 (0-2).

Going: Good or faster: 11911222 (4-8); G-S or softer: 587 (0-3).

Combine a distance between 5f and 7f, on good or faster ground and his record becomes: 1111222 (4-7) The first defeat coming when poorly drawn in a Group 1 at York, where he only went down by half-a-length to Kyllachy on his first 5f start. The two other defeats were narrow ones (both by just a short head).

MALHUB (USA)

MAMOUNIA (IRE)

Distance: 6f: 322 (0-3); 7f: 1210 (2-4); 8f: 821236 (1-6); 9f: 1 (1-1).

Going: Firm: 26 (0-2); G-F: 182131 (3-6); Good: 20 (0-2); G-S: 21 (1-2); Soft: 32 (0-2).

Fresh (seasonal debut): 31 (1-2).

Class: Group 2: 60 (0-2); Listed: 231 (1-3); Others: 322182211 (3-9).

Combine 7f-9f, below Group class and her record becomes: 182211231 (4-9). Her only poor run under these conditions, when eighth at Pontefract, can be forgiven as she ruined her chance by pulling too hard. Her trainer, Barry Hills, has an excellent record at Doncaster and Mamounia is unbeaten in two starts at that track.

MAMOUNIA (IRE)

MAMZACMA

Distance: 5f-12f: 0604107522047 (1-13); 13f+: 23211211 (4-8).

Going: G-F or faster: 341111 (4-6); Good: 0722 (0-4); G-S: 007 (0-3); Soft / Heavy: 622 (0-3); Fibresand: 41052 (1-5).

Combine a distance of 13f or further on good to firm or faster ground and his record becomes: 31111 (4-5). Three of these four wins were achieved at Newmarket where he has a record of three wins and a short head second from four starts at trips of 13f+. Although yet to win on soft ground he has finished second on it twice and should not be overlooked on such a surface, especially at Newmarket.

MANA D'ARGENT (IRE)

Distance: 6f-11f: 63327456303 (0-11); 12f-13f:13248222046520064287 (1-20); 14f-15f: 363950077 (0-9); 16f:+: 549313411045 (3-12).

Course: Ascot: 142263111 (4-9); Others: 633274563033234635989250045200642873 4077045 (0-43).

Combine a distance of 16f (two miles) or further at Ascot and his record becomes: 43111 (3-5). Both defeats came at Royal Ascot in the two-mile four-furlong Ascot Stakes. His Ascot record at two-miles only is: 111 (3-3).

MANA D'ARGENT (IRE)

MARSAD (IRE)

Distance: 5f: 3226 (0-4); 6f: 6340971331056433507200091202855655 61300800 (4-41); 7f: 8027 (0-4).

Going: G-F: 63320970202671000 (1-17); Good: 4356850201858 (1-13); G-S: 231405 30 (1-8); Soft: 6317092 (1-7); Heavy: 3056 (0-4).

Fresh *(first three starts of each season):* 633967133105500921713 (4-21).

Combine 6f, when fresh and his record becomes: 63397133105509113 (4-17). For his current trainer, Reg Akehurst, his record improves to: 97133105509113 (4-14). Not the best strike-rate but as his winning starting prices were 12-1, 7-1, 20-1 and 11-2 a healthy profit would have been returned by backing him under these conditions. He landed a huge gamble on his debut last season.

MARSAD (IRE)

MATERIAL WITNESS (IRE)

Distance: 6f: 2 (0-1); 7f: 32135412265173157 (3-17); 1m+: 230200520007722040366 (0-21).

Going: G-F+: 02621 (1-5); Good: 353205457 (0-9); G-S: 2220006123 (1-10); Soft / Heavy: 3106 (1-4); AWT: 77220403157 (1-11).

Field Size: 10+: 322302005320007220403654665173157 (2-33); 9-: 217122 (2-6).

Combine 7f on turf, in a small field (9 runners or fewer and his record becomes: 21122 (2-5). From left to right: 2nd (by a head), 1st , 1st , 2nd (by a short head) and 2nd (by a short head).

MATTY TUN

Distance: 5f: 466851281954316 (3-15); 6f: 0 (0-1).

Fresh (first two runs after a long break or when rested for 5 weeks+): 466851131 (3-9).

Trainer: J F Craze: 46068 (0-5); J Balding: 51281954316 (3-11).

Combine his 5f runs, when fresh, for his current trainer (John Balding) and his record becomes: 51131 (3-5). From left to right; 5th (of 18) on first start for his new stable, 1st, 1st, 3rd – did best of the low-drawn runners in a competitive Doncaster handicap (first five finishers drawn 14,15,6,19 and 16 of 22) and 1st.

MILLENNIUM FORCE

Distance: 6f: 6 (0-1); 7f: 120610133121 (5-12); 8f: 662433488 (0-9); 9f+: 8443 (0-4).

Going: G-F or faster: 68424318181 (3-11), Good: 31332 (1-5); G-S: 60460 (0-5); Soft / Heavy: 42316 (1-5).

Track: Straight: 204618011216 (4-12); Turning: 66844433123833 (1-14).

Combine a distance of 7f, on a straight track and his record becomes: 06101121 (4-8). From left to right; 17th – no chance from stall 30 at Newmarket (first six finishers drawn 3,7,10,4,1 and 2 of 27 (three non-runners)), 6th – badly hampered in the Victoria Cup at Ascot (would have been placed at least with a clear run), 1st – won at Lingfield despite poor stall one draw, 12th (promoted to 11th) – down the field in the Bunbury Cup at Newmarket (no obvious excuse), 1st, 1st, 2nd – only beaten by half-a-length in a 30-runner Newmarket handicap and 1st.

MILLENNIUM FORCE

MINDEROO

Distance: 5f: 0406 (0-4); 6f: 07610477251 (2-11); 7f+: 0578006 (0-7).

Going: G-F or faster: 001 (1-3); Good: no runs; G-S: 07400600 (0-8); Soft / Heavy: 7 (0-1); Fibresand: 5866477 (0-7); Polytrack: 251 (1-3).

Combine a distance of 6f, on a fast surface (good to firm or faster turf, or Polytrack) and his record becomes: 1251 (2-4). Both defeats were by a narrow margin. He has improved since joining Milton Bradley and it would be no surprise were his trainer to win a string of low-grade turf handicaps with him this season.

MONKSTON POINT (IRE)

Distance: 5f: 1313313020171301330 (5-19); 6f: 45699081007087143064192460 (3-27).

Going: G-F or faster: 339004 (0-6); Good: 456930940 (0-9); G-S: 1100830161 (4-10); Soft / Heavy: 13321171070708713034260 (5-21).

Time Of Year: March to mid-June: 1315691171301413 (8-17); Mid-June to November: 33413900208007087306340924600 ((1-29).

Overseas Runs: 9733926 (0-7).

Combine good to soft or softer ground when running in the UK before mid-June and his record becomes: 11111011 (7-8). The sole defeat was excusable as he was poorly drawn (stall one) in a big-field Doncaster handicap (the first four finishers were drawn in stalls 14,12,13 and 15 of 17 and raced on the opposite side of the track to Monkston Point).

MONKSTON POINT (left)

MURGHEM (IRE)

Distance: 8f-11f: 2582 (0-4); 12f-14f: 13224964137320222111112146 6052524371267 (8-38); 15f+: 2324005 (0-7).

Field Size: 13 or more runners: 8233306056 (0-10); 8-12 runners: 52223961724214 6025025 (2-21); 7 or fewer runners: 2144222111121243717 (6-18).

Combine a field of 12 or fewer runners, at distances between 12f and 14f and his record becomes: 1224964172222111112146252437127 (8-30). In fields of 7 runners or fewer his record improves to: 144221112143717 (6-15). As he has got older his form has declined but he is still capable of scoring at the right level. Last season he twice encounter a small field (12 or fewer runners), on turf, at a distance between 12f and 14f and in a race worth less than £10,000 to the winner; he won the first of them and finished second by a short head in the other.

MURGHEM (IRE)

MY BROTHER

Distance: 5f: 6067 (0-4); 6f: 12572770 (1-8); 7f: 0P790569 (0-8); 1m+: 905 (0-3).

Going: Firm: 79 (0-2); G-F: 09P505256707 (0-12); Good: 071602 (0-6); G-S: 76 (0-2); AWT: 9 (0-1).

Fresh (seasonal debut): 095122 (1-6).

Since joining his current trainer (Dr J R J Naylor) his seasonal debut record is: 122 (1-3). From left to right: 1st (33-1), 2nd – beaten by a neck (16-1) and 2nd – beaten by half-a-length (14-1). All three of these runs were at Goodwood and he would be a solid each-way bet if reappearing at the same track this season.

NEEDWOOD BLADE

Distance: 5f: 744 (0-3); 6f: 00112U0233111 (5-13); 7f: 1453520 (1-7); 8f: 0 (0-1).

Going: G-F or faster: 2105030144 (2-10); Good: 4U31 (1-4); G-S: 023 (0-3); Soft / Heavy: 711521 (3-6); Fibresand: 0 (0-1).

Fresh *(seasonal debut):* 702 (1-3).

Combine 6f, on turf, excluding seasonal debuts and his record becomes: 0112U033111 (5-11). From left to right: 10th – still in need of the experience when down the field on second ever start, 1st, 1st, 2nd – beaten by just half-a-length, U – unseated rider early on, 16th – poorly drawn in the Ayr Gold Cup, 3rd, 3rd, 1st, 1st and 1st.

NEEDWOOD BLADE

NEMO FUGAT (IRE)

Distance: 6f: 241301800 (2-9); 7f: 1000 (1-4).

Going: G-F: or faster: 2110018000 (3-10); Good: 40 (0-2); G-S: 3 (0-1).

Fresh *(absence since last race):* 42 days or more: 211 (2-3); 41 days or fewer: 413008 0000 (1-10).

Combine a distance of 6f or 7f, when running fresh (after a break of six weeks+) and his record becomes: 211 (2-3) with the sole defeat in a photo-finish (by a head). His only win when not fresh came in a weak Lingfield maiden for which he started the 4-11 favourite.

NEMO FUGAT (IRE)

NIGRASINE

Distance: 5f: 89 (0-2); 6f: 115242100344520210124240407741000019096673 (7-41); 7f: 73198333054876500 (1-17); 8f: 505900201850850180 (2-18); 9f+: 0 (0-1).

Going: Firm: 4173 (1-4); G-F: 11420852421076201980 (4-20); Good: 527501035919 42811230740809505610 (5-32); G-S: 34004030500 (0-11); Soft: 047098 (0-6); Heavy: 3 (0-1); AWT: 00850 (0-5).

Field Size: 20+: 200805450200073000000908500063 (0-29); 14-19: 280489769107180 (2-15); 10-13: 17904437501850 (2-14); 9-: 15245133914311224142 (6-21).

Class: A: 575919024243077 (1-15); B: 22008035445202830003040400880 (0-29); C: 14131145190769567 (5-17); D: 120150150000 (3-12); E-: 980318 (1-6).

Combine runs in class C or lower company. on good or faster ground and his record becomes: 11411110762019509150915731800 (9-25). In fields of 13 runners or fewer his figures improve to: 11411112150 (7-11). At 6f only they improve further to: 11411111 (7-8).

NORTHERN SVENGALI (IRE)

Distance: 5f: 0272222015503503021576900810315 080009407063000896040 (4-53) 6f: 201344407004003338347 (1-22), only win in a weak Catterick Maiden; 7f: 40609 (0-5).

Going: Firm: 2201358 (1-7); G-F: 22146945030100801000904 (3-23); Good: 02004040002504060090 (0-20); G-S: 2100790760 (1-10); Soft / Heavy: 747608 (0-6); AWT: 53533033383347 (0-14).

Class: C+: 200407000 (0-9); D: 02210443406950257900300760 (1-26); E: 72153530431608105803008 (3-23); F: 2201009403363834709040 (1-22).

Combine 5f, G-F or faster ground, in class E or lower company and his record becomes: 20318101580904 (3-14). When returned to the track within four days of his latest run this improves to: 311019 (3-6).

NORTHSIDE LODGE (IRE)

Distance: 10f: 76619711215124171112 (8-19); 12f: 986 (0-3).

Going: Firm: 12 (1-2); G-F: 69815411 (3-8); Good: 97 (0-2); G-S: 7627 (0-4); Polytrack: 11211 (4-5); Fibresand: 6 (0-1).

Combine 10f, on a fast surface (good to firm or faster turf, or Polytrack) and his record becomes: 611121514111112 (8-13). On firm turf or Polytrack only his strike-rate improves to: 1121112 (5-7) with the two defeats coming in photo-finishes (the first by a head, the second by just a short head).

OPTIMAITE

Going: Firm: 24 (0-2); G-F: 1000950501624231416 (4-19); Good: 11974086 (2-8); G-S: 4363 (0-4); Soft / Heavy: 9708 (0-4).

Field Size: 12 runners or more: 10009060703 (1-11); 7-11 runners: 493076942834867 (0-15); 6 runners or fewer: 12155124114 (5-11).

Fresh (first two runs each season): 11310138 (4-8).

Combine good or faster ground with a very small field (6 runners or fewer) and his record becomes: 12155124114 (5-11). When only considering his first two runs each season his small field, fast ground record improves to: 111 (3-3).

PALACE AFFAIR

Distance: 5f-6f: 5101902211180 (5-13); 7f: 215004 (1-6).

Ground: G-F or faster: 5009 (0-4); Good or softer: 510211024211180 (6-15).

Fresh (after a break of six weeks+): 50208 (0-5).

Class: Group 3: 00 (0-2); Listed: 1109024211180 (5-13); Others: 5125 (1-4).

Combine a distance of 6f or shorter, good or softer ground, excluding runs when fresh and her record becomes: 11221110 (5-8).

PALACE AFFAIR

PATAVELLIAN (IRE)

Distance: 6f: 1 (1-1); 7f: 0311 (2-4); 8f: 003 (0-3); 9f+: 032079 (0-6).

Going: G-F or faster: 0311 (2-4); Good: 200371 (1-6); G-S: 0 (0-1); Soft / Heavy: 30 (0-2); Polytrack: 9 (0-1).

Track: Straight: 003111 (3-6); Turning: 03203079 (0-8).

Combine a distance of 6f-7f, good or faster turf, on a straight track and his record becomes: 3111 (3-4). The sole defeat can be forgiven as he was poorly drawn in stall 1 on last season's reappearance at Salisbury (the first five finishers were drawn in stalls 11,15,1,10 and 14 of 19).

PATSY CULSYTH

Distance: 5f: 66522541324007830 (1-17); 6f: 2896020019604815900 (2-19); 7f+: 9100033006233200452 (1-19).

Going: Firm: 260850 (0-6); G-F: 6254008323200 (0-13); Good: 2413020010100 (3-13); G-S: 82917634 (1-8); Soft: 60090352 (0-8); Heavy: 349 (0-3); AWT: 5906 (0-4).

Class: Handicaps: 00200000973683004322590 5 (0-24); Claimers: 138990002 (1-9); Sellers: 5226116831300004 (3-15); Others: 6622544 (0-7).

Track: Newcastle: 230115 (2-6). Newcastle Sellers: 211 (2-3), only defeat by a short head.

Fresh *(seasonal debut):* 629100 (1-6).

Combine runs in selling company, at Newcastle and her record becomes: 211 (2-3) with the only defeat by just a short head.

She goes well fresh and won a Newcastle seller on her seasonal debut in March 2000 at odds of 33-1. Unfortunately her connections have wasted her last two debut runs by running her on Fibresand (2001) and over an inadequate five-furlong trip (2002).

PATSY CULSYTH

PAY THE SILVER

Distance: 5f-7f: 043554 (0-6); 8f: 60 (0-2); 8f 100y-9f: 228901314 (2-9); 10f: 5183608 7528470 (1-14); 11f+: 0005 (0-4).

Going: G-F or faster: 04552287123474 (1-14); Good: 3401001 (2-7); G-S: 8580 (0-4); Soft / Heavy: 5 (0-1); Fibresand: 6950 (0-4); Polytrack: 83060 (0-5).

Track: Epsom: 4515241 (2-7); Goodwood: 2013 (1-4).

Class: C+: 4840 (0-4); D: 0435620006003 (0-13); E: 5285193507152174 (3-16); F: 88 (0-2).

Combine a distance of 8f 100y to 10f, at Epsom or Goodwood, on good or faster ground, in class D company or lower and his record becomes: 211231 (3-6). From left to right: 2nd – poorly drawn in stall 1 at Goodwood (the first five finishers were berthed in stalls 14,1,9,12 and 11 of 14), 1st, 1st, 2nd – beaten in a photo-finish, 3rd – beaten in photo-finish, and 1st.

PEPPIATT

Distance: 5f: 560 (0-3); 6f: 1084433150056801000005330823090 06598620 (3-39); 7f+: 210733270676074855000294090857 (1-31).

Fresh *(absence since last race)*: 6 days or more: 12100847433270560 0568071500606050734835085306000029645989 08057 (3-62); 5 days or less: 33102509062 (1-11).

Combine a trip of 6f when racing 5 days or fewer since his last run and his record becomes: 33102962 (1-8). From left to right; 3rd (of 22) – beaten by half-a-length, 3rd (of 18) – beaten by half-a-length, 1st, 17th (of 18) – outclassed in Class B Goodwood handicap, 2nd (of 23) – beaten by a head, 9th (of 25) – unsuited by heavy ground, 6th (of 22) – heavy ground again, and 2nd (of 18) – beaten by a head.

PEPPIATT

PHECKLESS

Distance: 5f: 5 (0-1); 6f: 08000 (0-5); 7f: 2213021 (2-7); 8f: 3907 (0-4).

Going: G-F or faster: 100 (1-3); Good: 83 (0-2); G-S: 90 (0-2); Soft / Heavy: 0 (0-1); Fibresand: 570 (0-3); Polytrack: 322021 (1-6).

Fresh *(after a break of six weeks+)*: 053231 (1-6).

Combine 7f and a fast surface (good or faster turf, or Polytrack) and his record becomes: 2213021 (2-7). From left to right: 2nd – beaten just over one-length in a 14-runner field on Polytrack debut (10-1), 2nd – beaten by a head (8-1), 1st – won a

Southwell turf claimer (8-1), 3rd – did best of those drawn in double figures when a 33-1 shot for an Epsom handicap (the first four finishers were drawn in stalls 6,4,16 and 9 of 16), 14th – no chance from a poor low draw over Lingfield's straight seven furlong turf track, 2nd – beaten a length-and-a-half in a big field (25-1) and 1st – won on the Polytrack at Lingfield (11-1). He also goes well when fresh, winning after a 68-day break at Lingfield in February 2003.

PLEASURE TIME

Going: Firm: 12108 (2-5); G-F: 31227537573005187136781626 2000 (4-30); Good: 45950384512300 00890 (1-19); G-S: 5500000 (0-7); Soft / Heavy: 7227 (0-4); AWT: 0310048 (1-7).

Track: Flat: 45191278535710031210020030068180902310 2000048 (7-45); Undulations: 3553035457302572877107608 60 (1-27).

Fresh (absence since last race): 42 days or more: 43112083124 (3-11); 29-41 days: 9371060000 (1-10); 15-28 days: 3151055020328100307 18020 (4-24); 1-14 days or less: 5522785543770572070860960 08 (0-27).

Combine 5f, on a flat track, on G-F or faster ground (or an All-Weather track), when racing 15 days or more since last race and his record becomes: 1150011203612312 04 (6-18). Given a break of six weeks or more, on a flat track and on his favoured surface, his figures improve to: 1123124 (3-7).

POP THE CORK

Distance: 5f: 9837017008803167051133658008509 (4-31); 6f: 8 (0-1).

Going: Firm: 185 (1-3); G-F: 300316711368008509 (3-18); Good: 078053 (0-6); G-S: 70 (0-2); AWT: 988 (0-3).

Fresh *(first two runs each season or after a break of six weeks+):* 9883008658 (0-10).

Track: Musselburgh: 1115 (3-4).

Combine 5f at Musselburgh, on G-F or faster ground, excluding runs when fresh and his record becomes: 1115 (3-4), with the sole defeat excusable on account of a poor draw.

PROMPT PAYMENT (IRE)

Distance: 10f: 35421 (1-5); 11f-12f: 10116 (3-5).

Fresh *(seasonal debut):* 30 (0-2).

Combine a distance of 11f-12f, excluding seasonal debuts and her record becomes: 1116 (3-4). The sole defeat can be excused as she slipped on the home bend at Ascot.

PROUD BOAST

Distance: 5f: 103152629982013791 (4-18); 6f: 2000149 (1-7).

Going: G-F or faster: 02315290980143791 (3-17); Good: 201 (1-3); G-S: 102 (1-3); Soft / Heavy: 69 (0-2).

Field Size: 12 or more runners: 06290008201379 (1-14); 11 or fewer runners: 1231 5291491 (4-11).

Combine 5f, in a small field (11 or fewer runners) on G-S or faster ground and her record becomes: 13152911 (4-8). From left to right; 1st, 3rd – beaten by less than one length, 1st, 5th – fly-jumped the start (something she has done on more than one occasion) then hampered when making headway, 2nd – beaten less than one length by a subsequent Group 3 winner, 9th – lost all chance when swerving to the left on leaving the starting stalls, 1st and 1st.

She managed to win in a small field over six furlongs last season at York. However, she wouldn't be the first sprinter to only stay six at that track and she is far better suited by the minimum trip.

PROUD BOAST

QUALITAIR WINGS

Distance: 7f: 034710 (1-6); 8f: 0065663125444 (1-13); 9f+: 0 (0-1).

Going: G-F or faster: 063125 (1-6); Good: 34761 (1-5); G-S: 504 (0-3); Soft / Heavy: 0064 (0-4); AWT: 04 (0-2).

Track: Left-handed: 36035104 (1-8); Right-handed: 05624 (0-5); Straight: 0046714 (1-7).

He tends to hang to the left on straight tracks and although he won over Yarmouth's straight mile he's likely to be best suited to left-handed tracks (given a draw on or near a left-hand rail on a straight track would make him worthy of consideration too). His two outings at left-handed Catterick have seen him finish third at 50-1 (hampered twice and possibly unlucky) and win at odds of 6-1 (heavily backed from 10-1). Pay close attention to his Catterick runs this season.

RED CARNATION (IRE)

Distance: 6f-7f: 3355 (0-4); 8f: 12 (1-2); 10f: 14452 (1-5); 11f-12f: 434001 (1-6).

Going: G-F or faster: 5540 (0-4); Good: 312405 (1-6); G-S: no runs; Soft: 432 (0-3); Heavy: 3141 (2-4).

Combine a distance of 10f or further on soft or heavy going and her record becomes: 144321 (2-6). On heavy ground her strike-rate improves to: 141 (2-3).

RED CARNATION (IRE)

RED WINE

Distance: 6f-7f: 40 (0-2); 8f: 217271 (2-6); 10f: 4741 (1-4); 11f+: 3211 (2-4).

Going: G-F or faster: 23 (0-2); Good: 70741 (1-5); G-S: 71 (1-2); Soft / Heavy: 1 (1-1); Fibresand: 42112 (2-5); Polytrack: 4 (0-1).

Combine a distance of 10f or further, on G-S or softer ground and his record becomes: 11 (2-2).

The greater the emphasis on stamina, the better he performs. He rounded off last season with a 16-1 victory in the November Handicap at Doncaster (12f, heavy ground) and will be very interesting in soft ground handicaps this season.

RED WINE

REPERTORY

The runs discussed below are those in the UK only since the start of the 2000 season.

Distance: 5f: 703235718034841041801 (4-22); 6f: 044 (0-3).

Class: A: 0335848434084 (0-13); B: 701031 (2-6); C: 271410 (2-6).

Combine 5f runs, in class B or lower company and his record becomes: 72710314101 (4-11). From left to right; 7th – needed the run on his seasonal debut, 2nd – beaten half a length, 7th – injured his head in the starting stalls, 1st, 12th – poorly drawn in stall 2 of 19 at Ascot (seven of the first eight finishers were drawn in double figures), 3rd – needed the run on his seasonal debut, 1st, 4th – missed the break yet only beaten by a length and a quarter, 1st, 10th – poorly drawn on the outside at Beverley and 1st.

REPERTORY

ROSES OF SPRING

Distance: 5f: 027218480116 (3-12); 6f: 521522223000008029310 (2-21); 7f: 070 (0-3).

Field Size: 12+: 0222032070000080289300 (0-22); 11-: 51752221841116 (5-14).

Class: C: 000028006 (0-9); D: 0527522223200081 (1-16); E: 17024893111 (4-11).

Combine a distance of 5f or 6f, with a small field (11 runners or fewer) and her record becomes: 5152221841116 (5-13). In class D or lower company only her record improves to: 51522214111 (5-11). From left to right: 5th – badly hampered on second career start at Ripon, 1st, 5th – failed to stay 6f on soft ground at Newmarket , 2nd – only found the useful Torosay Spring too good in a valuable handicap at Lingfield, 2nd, 2nd, 1st, 4th, 1st, 1st and 1st.

ROXANNE MILL

Distance: 5f: 57346312470023432000619411106157700 (5-34); 6f: 00 (0-2).

Going: G-F or faster: 57323440615770 (1-14); Good: 603261 (1-6); G-S: 401 (1-3); Soft / Heavy: 30910 (1-5); Fibresand: 1247000 (1-7); Equitrack: 0 (0-1); Polytrack: no runs.

Field Size: 12 or more runners: 746000400061940657700 (1-20); 11 or fewer runners: 5331240723321117 (4-16).

Track: Nottingham: 3311 (2-4).

Combine a distance of 5f, on turf, in a small field (11 or fewer runners) and her record becomes: 53323211017 (3-11). On good or softer ground her strike-rate improves to: 33211 (2-5). She goes especially well at Nottingham and won two from two there last season, including one win in a big field.

ROXANNE MILL

SALIM TOTO

Distance: 8f-9f: 823 (0-3); 10f-11f: 22521 (1-5); 12f: 13811277 (3-8).

Going: G-F or faster: 31322227 (1-8); Good: 281 (1-3); G-S: 811 (2-3); Soft / Heavy: 57 (0-2).

Fresh *(first two runs each season or after a break of six weeks+):* 8212121 (3-7).

Combine a distance of 10f or further, on any ground, when running fresh and her record becomes: 12121 (3-5). She is two from two at Epsom and as a front-runner, goes especially well in small fields when allowed an uncontested lead.

SALIM TOTO

SARRAAF (IRE)

Field Size: 12 or more runners: 23500030010056P00744 (1-20); 9-11 runners: 23 (0-2); 8 or fewer runners: 4341811 (3-7).

Class: B: 008 (0-3); C: 23502303010 (1-11); D: 404056P074 (0-10); E: 1431 (2-4); F: 1 (1-1). Combine a small field (8 or fewer runners), in class E or lower company and his record becomes: 11 (2-2).

SEVEN NO TRUMPS

Distance: 5f: 15388010 (2-8); 6f: 0152022703800611350020 3100000 (4-29); 7f: 7 (0-1).

Going: Firm: 1 (1-1); G-F: 150381352000 (2-12); Good: 88001000 (1-8); G-S: 5232770 300 (0-10); Soft: 020610 (1-6); Heavy: 1 (1-1).

Fresh *(seasonal debut):* 0761 (1-4).

Class: A: 532770 (0-6); B: 5088350201 1000000 (2-17); C: 283006103 (1-9); D-: 011201 (3-6). Time of Year: March: 61 (1-2); April: 7 (0-1); May: 61171100 (4-8); June: 5503 (0-4); July: 85 (0-2); August: 23880000 (0-8); September: 0300200 (0-7); October: 223100 (1-6).

Combine a distance of 6f or shorter, in class B or lower company, excluding the summer months (June-August) and his record becomes : 1102001120310 (5-13). In the month of May only his strike-rate improves to: 11110 (4-5).

SEVEN NO TRUMPS

SIR DESMOND

Distance: 5f: 31132437304200090344208100 (3-26); 6f: 880688112 (2-9).

Going: Firm: 614 (1-3); G-F: 8332880448 (0-10); Good: 0137000 (1-7); G-S: 830432 011 (2-9); Soft / Heavy: 290 (0-3); Fibresand: 120 (1-3).

Course: Windsor: 2211 (2-4); Others: 880361132437830400009803440800120 (3-31).

He has only scored once from his last 24 outings away from Windsor and has developed into something of a course expert. His first defeat at the track was excusable on account of his moderate draw and the other reverse was a narrow one (by a head) in a field of 20 runners. He can be backed with confidence at Windsor this season, at distances of 5f or 6f, regardless of ground conditions.

SISTER-IN-LAW (FR)

Distance: 5f: 241510245 (2-9); 6f: 2 (0-1).

Going: G-F or faster: 2224 (0-4); Good: 05 (0-2); G-S: 15 (1-2); Soft / Heavy: 41 (1-2).

Fresh *(seasonal debut):* 24 (0-2).

Combine a distance of 5f, on good to soft or softer ground, excluding seasonal debuts and her record becomes: 151 (2-3). The sole defeat can be excused as she was unsuited by the switch in tactics from front running to being held-up.

SMOKIN BEAU

Distance: 5f: 431200036117017724017212 1268722 (7-31); 6f: 7353928090131211 (3-16).

Going: G-F+: 061240171312722 (4-15); Good: 431001216821 (4-12); G-S: 380721 (1-6); Soft / Heavy: 7927907 (0-7); AWT: 3153201 (2-7).

Field Size: 9 or more runners: 743313092800361079077240107121322682721 (6-39); 8 or fewer runners: 52111112 (5-8).

Combine a small field (8 or fewer runners), on turf and his record becomes: 111112 (5-6) – the sole defeat in a photo-finish.

SMOKIN BEAU

STARZAAN (IRE)

Distance: 8f-9f: 792 (0-3); 10f-12f: 105125 (2-6); 13f+: 34 (0-2).

Fresh *(first two runs each season or after a break of five weeks+):* 79211 (2-5); Others: 035254 (0-6).

Combine a distance of 10f-12f when running fresh and his record becomes: 11 (2-2).

STORMVILLE (IRE)

STORMVILLE (IRE)

Distance: 6f: 571 (1-3); 7f: 635620260615 (1-12); 8f+: 4086906430080 (0-13).

Track: Newcastle: 02171 (2-5); Others: 63556408269604603006580 (0-23).

Combine a distance of 6f-7f, when running at Newcastle and his record becomes: 2171 (2-4). From left to right: 2nd – did best of those to race on the unfavoured stands' side (seven furlongs), 1st (seven furlongs), 7th – did second best of those to race on the stands' side (six furlongs), and 1st (six furlongs).

TARA'S EMPEROR (IRE)

Distance: 5f: 4141599001170156009 (5-20); 6f: 9709271302 (1-10); 7f+: 900 (0-3).

Going: G-F: 990090030 (0-9); Good: 5700 (0-4); G-S: 409706 (0-6); Soft: 4192711509 (3-10); Heavy: 1112 (3-4).

Combine 5f, on soft or heavy ground and his record becomes: 411117150 (5-9). On heavy ground only his record improves to: 111 (3-3).

TEXAS GOLD

Distance: 5f: 211281533114420 (5-15); 6f: 65203 (0-5); 7f+: 0 (0-1).

Going: G-F or faster: 531144 (2-6); Good: 08332 (0-5); G-S: 0 (0-1); Polytrack: 62211 21 (3-7); Fibresand: 05 (0-2).

Field Size: 13 or more runners: 605208330 (0-9); 12 or fewer runners: 211231511442 (5-12).

Combine 5f on a fast surface (good to firm or faster turf, or Polytrack) and his record becomes: 21121531144 (5-11). He only once encountered a big field under these conditions, when beaten in a three-way photo-finish at Sandown (15 ran), and there is insufficient data to conclude that he cannot win in large fields.

THE BEST YET

Distance: 6f: 40371161 (3-8); 7f: 5601220 (1-7); 8f: 0 (0-1).

Going: Firm: 31 (1-3); G-F: 0 (0-1); Fibresand (standard): 5640002271 (1-10); Fibresand (slow): 6 (0-1); Polytrack: 11 (2-2).

Fresh (after a break of six weeks+): 500137116 (3-9).

Combine 6f-7f, when fresh, excluding runs on slow Fibresand and his record becomes: 5013711 (3-7). Ignoring all his runs on Fibresand his figures improve to: 131 (2-3).

THE TATLING (IRE)

Distance: 5f: 611208009960819218 (4-18); 6f: 3422632050213 (1-13).

Going: G-F or faster: 416300998192181 (4-15); Good: 3622020502 (0-10); G-S: 2063 (0-4); Soft: 18 (1-2).

Trainer: Michael Bell: 36412126203800 (2-14); David Nicholls: 20996081 (1-8); Milton Bradley: 952102813 (2-9).

He improved when stepped up to six furlongs last season and for the switch to Milton Bradley. His form for his new stable is worthy of closer inspection; 9th – missed the break over 5f, 5th (of 22) – doing third best of those to race on the unfavoured stands' side when a 50-1 shot for the Great St. Wilfrid Handicap at Ripon, 2nd, 1st, 10th – third best of the unfavoured far side in the Portland Handicap, 2nd – beaten by a neck in the Ayr Gold Cup (33-1) after being switched from a poor draw, 8th – poorly drawn over 5f at Ascot, 1st and 3rd – badly hampered twice and probably unlucky.

THE TATLING (right)

THE TRADER (IRE)

Distance: 5f: 32113402619316135814680 (6-23); 6f: 32470 (0-5); 7f: 0 (0-1).

Going: Firm: 2 (0-1); G-F: 211401115810 (6-12); Good: 3093468 (0-7); G-S: 3663 (0-4); Soft: 30247 (0-5).

Fresh *(seasonal debut):* 328 (0-3).

Headgear: Blinkers: 19316135814680 (3-14); Unblinkered: 332211340247069 (2-15).

Class: Group 1: 0 (0-1); Group 2: 454 (0-3); Group 3: 088 (0-3); Listed: 61316 (2-5); Others: 33221132470691931 (4-1).

Combine 5f, in Listed company or below, excluding seasonal debuts, when blinkered and his record becomes: 19311316 (4-8). On ground faster than good his figures improve to: 1111 (4-4).

THE TRADER

THE WHISTLING TEAL

Distance: 7f: 663 (0-3); 8f: 102127037015 (3-12); 9f: 520 (0-3); 10f: 2821514 (2-7); 12f: 2121 (2-4).

Going: G-F or faster: 102215212 (3-9); Good: 50001 (1-5); G-S: 3354 (0-4); Soft: 6638 71 (1-6); Heavy: 21 (1-2); AWT: 127 (1-3).

Field Size: 12 or more runners: 66310252870300152151 (5-21); 11 or fewer runners: 12374212 (1-8).

Trainer: J G Smyth-Osbourne: 663102512323703700 (2-18); Geoff Wragg: 15215142 121 (5-11).

Fresh *(after a break of six weeks+, for Geoff Wragg only):* 11421 (3-5).

Combine a distance of 10f or further on any ground (or shorter trips on heavy going), a big field (12 or more runners), since trained by Geoff Wragg and his record becomes: 121511 (4-6). From left to right; 1st – won a heavy ground mile-handicap at Pontefract (6-1), 2nd – finished strongly in a 10f Chester handicap after meeting trouble in running (6-1), 1st – won a firm ground Redcar handicap (9-4), 5th – badly hampered in 10f Ascot handicap yet still only beaten just over one length (7-2), 1st – won a York handicap by four lengths (7-1) and 1st – won the Group 3 St Simon Stakes at Newbury over 1f on soft ground (13-2). When considering only the runs after a break of six weeks or more his figures improve to: 111 (3-3).

THE WHISTLING TEAL

THORNTOUN GOLD (IRE)

Track: Windsor: 3111 (3-4).

He is a decent performer in minor handicap company and although he has won at other tracks he is included as a Windsor course expert. His Windsor record is: 3rd – beaten in a three-way photo-finish when a 16-1 shot, 1st (14-1), 1st (6-1) and 1st (9-2). All these runs took place at 10f-12f trips.

THUMPER (IRE)

Distance: 7f: 0222 (0-4); 8f: 78P20127 (1-8); 9f: 1 (1-1); 10f: 2 (0-2).

Going: G-F or faster: 8112 (2-4); Good: 27 (0-2); G-S: 022 (0-3); Soft / Heavy: 7P (0-2); Polytrack: 225 (0-3); Fibresand: 0 (0-1).

Fresh *(absence since last race):* 42 days or more: 70P20 (0-5); 15-41 days: 8225 (0-4); 14 days or less: 221127 (2-6).

Headgear: Blinkers: 21257 (1-5); Without: 780P202221 (1-10).

Combine a distance in excess of 7f, on good to firm or faster turf, after a recent run (14 days or less since his latest start) and his record becomes: 112 (2-3). At distances between 8f and 9f only his figures improve to: 11 (2-2).

THUNDERING SURF

Distance: 8f: 57 (0-2); 10f: 81354324242 (1-11); 12f: 61313600631 (3-11).

Going: G-F or faster: 834263063 (0-9); Good: 715442111 (4-9); G-S: 56 (0-2); Soft / Heavy: 3230 (0-4).

Track: Left-handed: 332230 (0-6); Right-handed: 815444261360631 (4-16); Straight: 57 (0-2).

Combine a distance of 10f-12f, good ground, on a right-handed track and his record becomes: 1544111 (4-7). The only unplaced effort came as a result of him being badly hampered (twice) at Kempton. At 12 furlongs only his good ground right-handed track record improves to: 111 (3-3).

THUNDERING SURF

TOLDYA

Distance: 5f-5f 110y: 80213469314187 (3-14); 5f 111y – 6f: 72232155645751704732 3 1820 (3-25); 7f: 429 (0-3); 8f: 8 (0-1).

Going: G-F or faster: 8027421712 (2-10); Good: 4645953838 (0-10); G-S: 77 (0-2); Soft / Heavy: 1637 (1-4); Fibresand: 31080 (1-5); Equitrack: 22432155 (1-8); Polytrack: 2941 (1-4).

Field Size: 13 or more runners: 8024165457953729074383 1820 (2-26); 12 or fewer runners: 72243213561481217 (4-17).

Combine a distance of 5f-6f, in a small field (12 or fewer runners) on good to firm or faster turf or an artificial surface and her record becomes: 2232135141217 (4-13). Her turf record under these conditions is: 217 (1-3). From left to right: 2nd – beaten in a photo-finish at Newmarket, 1st – won a class C Newcastle handicap and 7th – missed the break and forced to switch wide for a run at Epsom. She tends to drift left in her races and will always be suited by running on or near a left-hand running rail. She is capable of winning in a big field if the runners split into two or more distinct groups. This situation occurred at Kempton last season when she made all the running up the stands' side rail from a group of 8-runners.

TOMMY SMITH

Distance: 5f: 7641600420081010000110 1U859 (6-27); 6f: 15602006 (1-8).

Going: Good or faster: 74116502420081010000111U6859 (7-28); G-S or softer: 8060 000 (0-7).

Field Size: 13 or more runners: 6024081001000001069 (3-19); 12 or fewer runners: 784116500201 1U85 (4-16).

Time Of Year: June: 84112420011 (4-11); July: 6508101U (2-8); August: 0001 (1-4); Other Months: 706000006859 (0-12).

Headgear: Blinkers: 06859 (0-5); Visor: 010010001101U (5-13); No Headgear: 78411650602420080 (2-17).

Combine 5f, on good or faster ground, in the months of June to August, when wearing headgear and his record becomes: 101111U (5-7). He has only lost twice under these conditions with both defeats excusable; the "duck-egg" can be ignored as his saddle slipped, and he unseated his rider in the other. His only wins without headgear came in sellers when a two-year-old.

TOMTHEVIC

Distance: 5f: 47211009673254300500706212700 (3-29); 6f: 3000862686 (0-10).

Going: G-F or faster: 321010096230865270621206 (3-24); Good: 735068 (0-6); G-S: 0740 (0-4); Soft / Heavy: 400 (0-3); Fibresand: 70 (0-2).

Track: Straight: 31010009673243865027021278 07 (3-28); Turning: 47205000660 (0-11).

Time of Year: February: 0 (0-1); April: 0 (0-1); May: 00500 (0-5); June: 409627 (0-6); July: 7327306 (0-7); August: 101254306212 (3-12); September: 860780 (0-6); October: 6 (0-1).

Combine a straight five furlongs, on good or faster ground, in August, and his record becomes: 1123212 (3-7). From left to right: 1st, 1st, 2nd by a neck, 3rd – first home on the unfavoured stands' side at Musselburgh (the first three finishers were drawn in stalls 17,13 and 5 of 17), 2nd – finding only the in-form Sunley Sense (a winner on his previous and subsequent start) too good, 1st and 2nd by a short head.

TOM TUN

Distance: 5f: 5518132000531210901 (5-19); 6f:811761131464451243 7265230911 0062 1050863233160120041 (12-50); 7f+: 00054 (0-5).

Going: G-F or faster: 05151220010000 (3-14); Good: 13443590500660 (1-14); G-S: 81 6381124 (3-9); Soft: 0640701 0211 (3-11); Heavy: 91 (1-2); AWT: 15718113265203612 1354233 (6-24).

Course: Doncaster: 1139211 (4-7).

His three turf wins at 5f were all recorded on tracks with stiff uphill finishes (Leicester, Newcastle and Pontefract) and he has proved ineffective at the minimum trip on flat tracks, even on heavy ground. Combine good to soft or softer ground with a distance of 6f (or 5f on a stiff track) and his record becomes: 8614307010218112141 (7-19). For his current trainer (James Given) his figures improve to: 112141 (4-6). From left to right: 1st (Doncaster class C handicap), 1st (Ayr class D handicap), 2nd (beaten by a neck in a valuable (£32k to the winner) handicap at the Curragh), 4th (beaten two lengths in Newbury class B handicap) and 1st (won a Listed race at Doncaster).

He usually starts the turf season in the Town Moor Handicap at his favoured Doncaster. However, he's rated too high for that 0-90 event but the Listed Cammidge Trophy at the same meeting would make an ideal early season target.

TOM TUN

TOTEM POLE

Distance: 6f: 0005 (0-4); 7f: 324 (0-3); 8f: 104 (1-3); 9f: 6 (0-1).

Going: G-F or faster: 004465 (0-6); Good: 2 (0-1); G-S: 0310 (1-4).

Fresh (absence since last race): 35 days or more: 0312 (1-4); 34 days or fewer: 0004465 (0-7).

Combine a distance of 7f or further, when fresh and his record becomes: 312 (1-3).
From left to right: 3rd – tenderly ridden when a 16-1 shot on last season's reappearance, 1st – won his maiden at Haydock (11-4) and 2nd – narrowly beaten in an Epsom handicap (9-1).

TRANSATLANTIC (USA)

Distance: 7f: 54 (0-2); 8f: 61107 (2-5); 9f: 100 (1-3); 10f: 40 (0-2); 11f+: 0 (0-1).

Going: G-F or faster: 4640 (0-4); Good: 110 (2-3); G-S: 500 (0-3); Soft / Heavy: 170 (1-3).

Fresh (after a break of four weeks+): 5110170 (3-7).

Track: Left-handed: 0 (0-1); Right-handed: 4614110070 (3-10); Straight: 50 (0-2).

Combine runs on a right-handed track, when fresh and his record becomes: 111 (3-3).

TRANSATLANTIC

TURTLE VALLEY (IRE)

Distance *(flat runs only):* Under 12f: 962764506 (0-9); 12f-13f: 221707000 (1-9); 14f: 11012447 (3-8); 15f+: 8547236005605 (0-13).

Going *(jumps and flat combined):* Good or faster: 96276402618764470 (1-17); G-S or softer: 21154037023411416005250 (5-23); AWT: 5700 (0-4).

Field size *(jumps and flat combined):* 13+: 9066006470000 (0-13); 12-: 62764522111875 40377023411415245 (6-31)

Track *(UK flat runs only):* Undulations: 2280005405 (0-10); Flat: 9676452611147723l6 02647000 (4-26).

Combine a distance of 12f-14f, in a small field (12 runners or fewer), on G-S or softer ground and his record becomes: 21170012 (3-8). On flat tracks only this improves to: 1112 (3-4). He only encountered his ideal conditions once last season and did as well as could be expected by finishing second on unfavourable terms in a Doncaster conditions race. He conceded 13lb to the odds-on winner but would have been getting 27lb in a handicap.

TURTLE VALLEY (IRE)

TWICE UPON A TIME

Distance: 5f-5f16ly: 23134340 (1-8); 6f: 2440070 (0-7).

Going: Firm: 13434 (1-5); G-F: 400 (0-3); Good: 2407 (0-4); G-S: 23 (0-2); Soft: 0 (0-1).

Fresh *(absence since last run):* 42 days or more: 21 (1-2); 28-41 days: 30 (0-2); 27 days or fewer: 44023037440 (0-11).

A record of one win from 15 starts is hardly inspiring but her ideal conditions, namely G-F or faster ground after a lay-off, have only coincided the once, when she won at odds of 10-1 on her reappearance last season. Pay close attention to her debut this term, especially if she reappears at Bath.

UNSHAKABLE (IRE)

Distance: 7f: 1 (1-1); 8f: 52183 (1-5); 9f: 2 (0-1).

Going: G-F or faster: 11 (2-2); Good: 8 (0-1); G-S: 3 (0-1); Soft: 522 (0-3).

Fresh *(absence since last race):* 35 days or more: 5112 (2-4); 34 days or less: 283 (0-3).

His best efforts have come when fresh: 5112 (2-4). From left to right: 5th – needed the experience on his racecourse debut but still ran well in a 26-runner field when a 66-1 shot, 1st, 1st and 2nd – beaten by a short head. He is unbeaten in two starts on fast ground but also handles a soft surface.

VITA SPERICOLATA (IRE)

Distance: 5f: 1251359024834252714048000067 (3-27); 6f: 63843100912250 (2-14); 7f: 8 (0-1).

Going: Firm: 1 (1-1); G-F: 53593474140025670 (1-17); Good: 21483852310091 (3-14); G-S: 6040 (0-4); Soft: 2802 (0-4); Heavy: 28 (0-2).

Field Size: 12 or more runners: 59604582704000267 (0-17); 11 or fewer runners: 121 352833842431104809
1250 (4-25).

Class: A: 51359602488458731448000912670 (3-29); B: 2300025 (0-7); C: 32241 (1-5); D-: 1 (1-1). The problem with breaking down class in this way is that it doesn't differentiate between a £10,000 Listed race and a £100,000 Group race, as they are both Class A events. Using race value instead, a clearer picture of Vita Spericolata's class barrier emerges:

Race Value to Winner: £19,000+: 559604838470480002270 (0-21); Under £19,000: 121323258243110409156 (5-21).

Combine a small field (11 or fewer runners), good or faster ground, in races worth less than £19,000 to the winner and her record becomes: 121334311915 (5-12)

VITA SPERICOLATA (IRE)

WAHJ (IRE)

Distance: 6f: 070 (0-3); 7f: 13401120151 0362976060 (5-21); 1m: 18924870 (1-8).

Going: G-F or faster: 110101787560 (4-12); Good: 92039760 (0-8); G-S: 834014120 (2-9); Soft / Heavy: 6 (0-1); AWT: 20 (0-2).

Field size: 13 or more runners: 009202850307000 (0-15); 12 or fewer runners: 11834 111747162966 (6-17).

Combine 7f, G-S or faster ground, a small field (12 or fewer runners) and his record becomes: 113411112966 (6-12). On good to firm or faster ground only his figures improve to: 11116 (4-5).

WAHJ (IRE)

WAIT FOR THE WILL (USA)

Going: G-F or faster: 13622313798061 11234 (5-19); Good: 5601005832 (1-10); G-S: 5000 (0-4); Polytrack: 312 (1-3).

Track: Left-handed: 5062075312323 (1-13); Right-handed: 56130001231309806811214 (6-23).

Combine good to firm or faster ground, on a right-handed track and his record becomes: 13231398061114 (5-14).

WELSH EMPEROR (IRE)

Distance: 5f: 331360260 (1-9); 6f: 130295151 3-9); 7f: 222 (0-3).

Going: G-F or faster: 329 (0-3); Good: 23023026 (0-8); G-S: 3160 (1-4); Soft: 152 (1-3); Heavy: 151 (2-3).

Combine runs at any trip, on officially soft or heavy ground and his record becomes: 151251 (3-6). From left to right; 1st – made all over 5f at Catterick. 5th – missed the break over 6f at Ripon on ground only rated as yielding by Raceform, 1st – made all on heavy ground at Haydock (6f), 2nd – beaten by a short head at Leicester where the 7f trip on a stiff track proved a shade too far, 5th – did best of those to race on the slower far side at Doncaster (6f, heavy) and 1st – won a Listed race over 6f at Maisons-Laffitte despite missing the break.

Six furlongs on heavy ground are likely to be his optimum conditions and he can make his mark in Group company this season.

ZUHAIR

XANADU

Going: Firm: 1112100027 (4-10); G-F: 78031012430201505073 (3-20); Good or softer: 05570006000056000015 (1-21).

Fresh (absence since last run days): 31 days or longer: 0500000 (0-7); 8-30 days: 57803010123620000005500050727 (2-29); 7 days or fewer: 171121405160613 (6-15).

Combine runs on G-F or faster ground, with a very recent run (7 days or fewer since his last start) and his record becomes: 17112140103 (5-11). On firm ground only this improves to: 1112 (3-4), with the sole defeat by just a short head.

ZUHAIR

Distance: 5f: 07074214180000093100759315000004197 (4-34); 6f: 31517365302002286400520046071910070359571800453290090852009 (5-59); 7f+: 900 (0-3).

Going: Firm: 0400 (0-4); G-F: 3153026211100197455321952097 (6-28); Good: 735002 760000791070003355719390050804109 (3-39); G-S: 20457400090 (0-11); Soft: 8088 000 (0-7); Heavy: 0 (0-1); AWT: 916204 (1-6).

Course: Goodwood: 5110155143190120 (6-16).

Combine a distance of 5f, at Goodwood and his record becomes: 1111 (4-4).

All four wins came in the same race, the Charlton Stakes at the Glorious Goodwood Festival (in 1999, 2000, 2001 and 2002. Don't rule out a five-timer this season.

FORM BREAKERS UPDATE ORDER FORM

£5.00 each
£8.00 for any two
£10.00 for all three

Available by post or email

Royal Ascot 2003 ❏

Updates for the Form-Breakers to have run so far, plus new additions. Big race previews for the Royal meeting.

Glorious Goodwood ❏

Updates for the Form-Breakers to have run so far, plus new additions. Big race previews for the Glorious Goodwood festival.

September Special ❏

Updates for the Form-Breakers to have run so far, plus new additions. Big race previews, including the Ayr Gold Cup.

I enclose a cheque / postal order value £_____ made payable to Andrew Mount. Please send to Andrew Mount, PO Box 6745, Market Harborough, Leicestershire, LE16 9WT.

PLEASE TICK RELEVANT BOXES ABOVE.

Name_____

Address_____

_____Post Code_____

Email (if applicable)_____

A Trend Horses private daily subscription service is also available. Please contact andy.mount@ntlworld.com for more details or write to the address above.